BTEC Level 2 First Study Skills Guide in Travel and Tourism

Welcome to your Study Skills Guide! You can make it your own – start by adding your personal and course details below...

Learner's name: _____

BTEC course title: _____

Date started: _____

Mandatory units:

_____

_____

_____

Optional units:

_____

_____

_____

Centre name: _____

Centre address: _____

_____

_____

Tutor's name: _____

Published by Pearson Education Limited, a company incorporated in England and Wales, having its registered office at Edinburgh Gate, Harlow, Essex, CM20 2JE. Registered company number: 872828

Edexcel is a registered trademark of Edexcel Limited

Text © Pearson Education Limited 2010

First published 2010

13 12 11 10
10 9 8 7 6 5 4 3 2 1

British Library Cataloguing in Publication Data
A catalogue record for this book is available from the British Library

ISBN 978 1 84690 567 4

Typeset and edited by DSM Partnership
Cover design by Visual Philosophy, created by eMC Design
Cover photo/illustration © Masterfile
Printed in Malaysia, KHL-CTP

Acknowledgements
The author and publisher would like to thank the following individuals and organisations for permission to reproduce photographs:
Alamy Images: Marvin Dembinsky Photo Associates 81, David R. Frazier Photolibrary, Inc 41, Ace Stock Limited 60; Corbis: 66, Comstock 5; Getty Images: Tim Hall / Digital Vision 43; iStockphoto: Olena Dyachenko 85, Masaru Horie 81/2, 81/3, 82/2, 82/3, 83, 84/2, 84/3, 85/2, 85/3, 86, 86/2, Lucía de Salterain 84, Jess Wiberg 82; Pearson Education Ltd: Image100. Alamy 46, Steve Shott 24, Ian Wedgewood 37; TopFoto: John Powell 20.

All other images © Pearson Education

Every effort has been made to contact copyright holders of material reproduced in this book. Any omissions will be rectified in subsequent printings if notice is given to the publishers.

Websites
Go to www.pearsonhotlinks.co.uk to gain access to the relevant website links and information on how they can aid your studies. When you access the site, search for either the title BTEC Level 2 First Study Skills Guide in Travel and Tourism or ISBN 9781846905674.

Disclaimer
This material has been published on behalf of Edexcel and offers high-quality support for the delivery of Edexcel qualifications.
This does not mean that the material is essential to achieve any Edexcel qualification, nor does it mean that it is the only suitable material available to support any Edexcel qualification. Edexcel material will not be used verbatim in setting any Edexcel examination or assessment. Any resource lists produced by Edexcel shall include this and other appropriate resources. Copies of official specifications for all Edexcel qualifications may be found on the Edexcel website: www.edexcel.com

Contents

Popular progression pathways

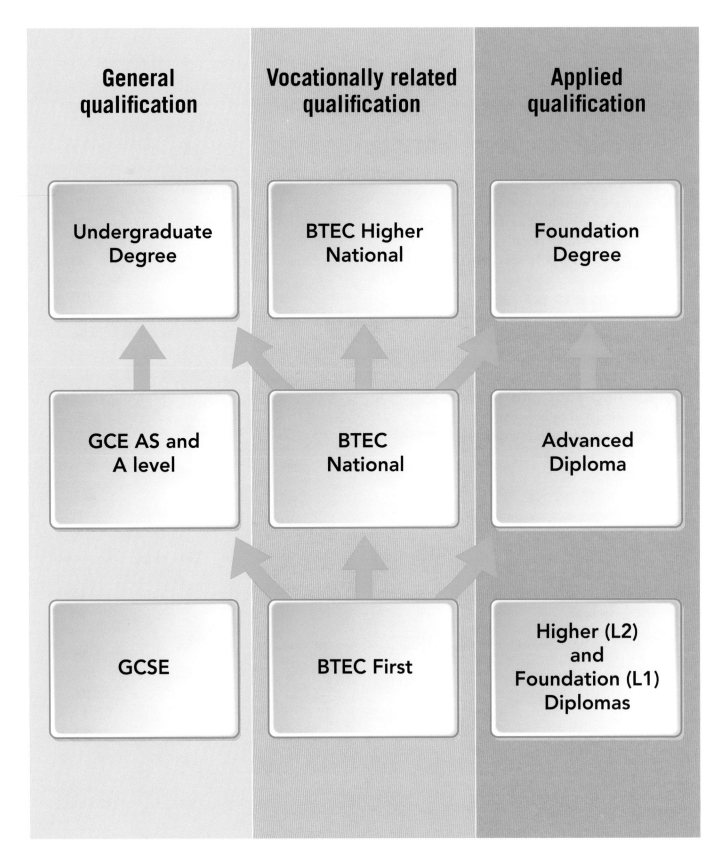

Your BTEC First course
Early days

Every year many new learners start BTEC Level 2 First courses, enjoy the challenge and successfully achieve their award. Some do this the easy way; others make it harder for themselves.

Everyone will have different feelings when they start their course.

Case study: Starting a new course

Lauren prepares to begin her BTEC Travel and Tourism course.

'Moving from primary school to secondary school seemed like a big step, and I can remember feeling a little bit anxious about what it was going to be like. I need not have worried because it turned out to be fine. However, that feeling of anxiety has started to come back again and I don't know why, because I've been really looking forward to starting my BTEC First in Travel and Tourism.

'Maybe it's because none of my friends has chosen this course. I'm used to being part of a small crowd, so it's going to seem strange starting the course on my own. However the course really appealed to me because working as part of the travel and tourism industry sounds very exciting and I'd like to work overseas in the future.

'My teacher said that it's normal to feel apprehensive when moving on to do something different. He talked about stepping outside your comfort zone and how it is good to have to deal with new things because that's what will happen throughout life.

'He gave me some good tips and said that I should try and turn negative thoughts into positive ones.

'For example, instead of a negative thought like, "I don't know anyone on the course, what if I don't like them?", I should think, "I've always made friends easily, so why should this be any different?" If I do eventually go to work overseas, I would have to deal with this on a much bigger scale, so the more confidence I build up now the better.

'I'm sure that with this approach, I will be fine.'

Do you have any concerns about starting your BTEC First in Travel and Tourism?

About your course

What do you know already?

If someone asks you about your course, could you give a short, accurate description? If you can, you have a good understanding of what your course is about. This has several benefits.

Four benefits of understanding your course

1. You will be better prepared and organised.
2. You can make links between the course and the world around you.
3. You can check how your personal interests and hobbies relate to the course.
4. You will be alert to information that relates to topics you are studying, whether it's from conversations with family and friends, watching television, or at a part-time job.

Read any information you have been given by your centre. You can also check the Edexcel website www.edexcel.com for further details.

Interest/hobby	How this relates to my studies

What else do you need to know?

Five facts you should find out about your course

1. The type of BTEC qualification you are studying.
2. How many credits your qualification is worth.
3. The number of mandatory units you will study and what they cover.
4. How many credits the mandatory units are worth.
5. The number of optional units you need to study in total and the options available in your centre.

Case study: Course decisions

Gina is 14 and has chosen to study for a BTEC First Certificate in Travel and Tourism at school. She thinks she would like to work in the travel industry but has decided that it would be sensible to keep her options open, so she will take GCSEs alongside the BTEC First. Gina is going to continue with her language GCSEs because these could be useful if she does eventually work in travel and tourism in the future.

Her cousin Isaac is 16 and he has just started a BTEC First Diploma in Travel and Tourism at a local further education college. Isaac did reasonably well in his GCSEs but could have done better in some subjects. By taking a BTEC First over one year he hopes that he will be able to progress to the BTEC National in Travel and Tourism. He is also going to re-sit his Maths GCSE to try and improve his grade.

Gina and Isaac get together to compare the courses they are taking. They find that some of the units are exactly the same, although Isaac will be studying more units than Gina and will have the opportunity to gain more credits. Isaac has more classes each week for his travel and tourism course.

Gina likes working with people and is interested in the customer service side which involves working with people. Isaac knows this is important, and he will also complete a customer service unit, but his real interest is in the operational side of the business and he is looking forward to learning about different destinations and planning holidays.

What are you most looking forward to on your BTEC First in Travel and Tourism?

TRY THIS

Find out which optional units your centre offers. To check the topics covered in each unit go to www.edexcel.com.

TOP TIPS

If you have a choice of optional units in your centre and are struggling to decide, talk through your ideas with your tutor.

Activity: How well do you know your course?

Complete this activity to check that you know the main facts. Compare your answers with a friend. You should have similar answers except where you make personal choices, such as about optional units. Your tutor can help you complete number 9.

1 The correct title of the BTEC award I am studying is:

2 The length of time it will take me to complete my award is:

3 The number of mandatory units I have to study is:

4 The titles of my mandatory units, and their credit values, are:

5 The main topics I will learn in each mandatory unit include:

Mandatory unit	Main topics

6 The number of credits I need to achieve by studying optional units is:

7 The titles of my optional units, and their credit values, are:

8 The main topics I will learn in each optional unit include:

Optional unit	Main topics

9 Other important aspects of my course are:

10 After I have achieved my BTEC First, my options include:

Introduction to the travel and tourism sector

Welcome to the dynamic world of travel! There are millions of employees working in the travel and tourism sector around the world, and there are many exciting job opportunities to attract people with different skills and qualities.

The BTEC First in Travel and Tourism will open up the world of travel to you. You will investigate different destinations at home and abroad, learn how to make routine travel arrangements for coach and rail trips, and also plan holidays. You will see that the travel and tourism sector is made up of many organisations that work together to provide and market a wide range of services to meet the needs of different kinds of people.

Excellent customer service makes a travel and tourism organisation stand out from its competitors. Employers are keen to recruit staff who put the customer first, and your people skills will be developed to help to prepare you for working in travel and tourism.

If you have taken a holiday in the past, or been on a school or college trip, you will have experienced travel and tourism services at first hand. For example, you may have taken an overseas holiday or know someone who has travelled abroad on holiday. You may be surprised to learn how many people will have been involved in making sure that holidays are enjoyable and that all arrangements run smoothly.

In the space below, make a list of some of the people you think would be involved in an overseas holiday and outline their main roles.

Did you think of any of these jobs?

Travel agent	Helps you select the right holiday and makes your booking
Airport check-in staff	Checks in your luggage, confirms your seat and checks your documentation
Cabin crew	Looks after you during the flight, serves meals and refreshments
Holiday representative	Meets you at the airport, provides information, sells excursions, sorts out problems
Hotel receptionist	Checks you into your room, provides information, sorts out problems

Your course will introduce you to many career opportunities in the travel and tourism sector.

What types of travel and tourism jobs appeal to you?

Case study: Nathan's introduction to the industry

Nathan completed his BTEC First in Travel and Tourism in 2007 and now works as a travel consultant for a leading tour operator.

'There is something about the travel industry that just appealed to me. Whenever I went on holiday and saw the holiday representatives in action I would think "That's the job for me". I took my first step towards this goal by signing up for the BTEC First in Travel and Tourism. This gave me an excellent overview of the travel and tourism industry and made me realise that it is much bigger than I had thought.

'During the course I had the chance to develop many skills and gain valuable work experience. I took part in day trips and residential visits and I began to realise what goes on behind the scenes. All of these things gave me confidence, and confirmed to me that I wanted to pursue a career in travel and tourism.

'After completing the BTEC First I decided to progress to the BTEC National Diploma in Travel and Tourism and was very pleased to pass this in 2009. I am currently working as a travel consultant and am putting my studies to good use. I feel that this is a good career move – I am only 18 and I think that a year or two of building up my knowledge and further developing my customer service skills will be a great addition to my travel and tourism qualifications.

'The organisation I work for has opportunities both abroad and in the UK and will actively help me to achieve my goal of working overseas as a holiday representative in a year or two. They have opportunities for cabin crew and tour operations too. Overall I think this is a great start to my career in travel and tourism.'

Would you like to follow in Nathan's footsteps?

Skills you need for the travel and tourism sector

When completing the mandatory and optional units on the BTEC First in Travel and Tourism you will have the opportunity to develop a range of skills.

Customer service

Travel and tourism has many job roles where the customer is the main focus, therefore customer service skills are very important.

Customer-facing roles include:

- cabin crew
- airport check-in staff
- holiday representatives
- retail travel agents
- hotel receptionists
- tourist information officers
- tour guides
- booking office staff
- ride attendants.

Keeping the customer happy is very important in travel and tourism and there are many different skills that come together under the umbrella of 'customer service'.

- **Communication skills**

  Knowing how to communicate effectively with customers is a valuable skill. This is not just what you say, but how you say it. Providing the right information at the right time and in the right way forms the basis of good communication skills.

  Face-to-face communication skills are needed, for example, when:

  - providing information to visitors
  - giving directions
  - selling a product or service
  - calming people down when something goes wrong
  - giving instructions.

- **Written communication skills**

  Accurate written communications create a positive impression of a company. If letters and other written materials are full of mistakes, they would give a bad impression, and if they contained inaccurate information, they could ruin someone's travel plans.

  Written communications include:

  - itineraries
  - letters
  - emails
  - reports
  - material on notice boards and displays.

- **Telephone skills**

  Many travel and tourism organisations conduct business over the telephone. Some have large call centres where hundreds of staff are employed to make sales and provide information over the telephone. Poor telephone technique could lose sales and business.

- **Presentation skills**

  Many roles in travel and tourism are in the public eye. Cabin crew, for example, have to make safety announcements, while holiday representatives make welcome presentations to their guests.

- **Complaint handling skills**

  Sometimes things do go wrong on package holidays and with other travel and tourism services. Being able to deal with complaints effectively is a skill, and it can make the difference between a dissatisfied and a satisfied customer.

- **Listening skills**

  Not many people think of listening as a skill. However, it is very important in the travel and tourism sector. Sales consultants need to listen to customer requests so that they can suggest products and services to meet their needs.

- **Selling skills**

  Customers do not always know exactly what they want, and it is a skill to turn an enquiry into a sale.

  There are many parts of the travel and tourism sector where selling skills are important. For example, they are required when selling:

  – package holidays

  – tickets for an attraction

  – excursions to holidaymakers.

IT skills

Technology is used extensively by most travel and tourism organisations. For example, travel and tourism organisations have IT systems:

- to make bookings
- to find information
- to communicate
- to produce reports
- to store data.

Being computer literate has become an everyday expectation, and using technology will be a necessary skill in many jobs. Business travel agents, for example, rely heavily on technology for making business travel arrangements.

Language skills

Being able to speak another language is not usually essential, but it can be useful for some jobs in travel and tourism. Large hotels like to employ multilingual staff to help their guests, while local guides may provide a service in different languages. If you work as a holiday representative, you may find it useful to have some language skills when working overseas.

Administrative skills

Not all jobs in travel and tourism involve dealing with the public. There are many jobs behind the scenes, where administrative tasks have to be carried out accurately and efficiently, especially in the offices of large organisations like tour operators. These can involve maintaining customer records and files.

Teamwork

Whichever part of the travel and tourism sector you work in, you are likely to find teams working together. For example, it might be:

- the crew on board a flight
- the staff in a local travel agency
- the tour representatives on a holiday
- the ride attendants at a visitor attraction
- the different teams of staff in a hotel, such as reception, bar, restaurant and housekeeping staff.

Being able to work effectively as part of a team is a skill that most employers look for. Teamwork is one area of the personal, learning and thinking skills (PLTS) that you will develop while you are completing your BTEC programme.

Review the last two pages on skills. Which are your strongest skills?

More about BTEC Level 2 Firsts

What is different about a BTEC Level 2 First?

How you learn

Expect to be 'hands-on'. BTEC Level 2 Firsts are practical and focus on the skills and knowledge needed in the workplace. You will learn new things and learn how to apply your knowledge.

BTEC First learners are expected to take responsibility for their own learning and to be keen and well-organised. You should enjoy having more freedom, while knowing you can still ask for help or support if you need it.

How you are assessed

Many BTEC First courses are completed in one year, but if you are taking GCSEs as well, you may be doing it over two years or more. You will be assessed by completing **assignments** written by your tutors. These are based on **learning outcomes** set by Edexcel. Each assignment will have a deadline.

Case study: Course assessment

Rhian is attending a taster day at the local college and is keen to find out how the assessments work on the BTEC First Travel and Tourism programmes. Some of the current learners are on hand as 'buddies', so she asks Joe, her buddy for the day, if he has found the work hard and if it is very different to things he had done before. This is his response.

'For each of the units we take, we are given assignments, and these are broken down into different tasks. We can see clearly what we have to do to gain pass, merit or distinction grading criteria for each assignment.

'The first unit we studied was on the UK travel and tourism sector. For our first assignment we were set a scenario in which we were travel journalists who had to investigate the different types of organisations that make up the UK travel and tourism sector. We had a talk from a tourism officer, who told us about the travel organisations in our area. We also visited a hotel and a coach company to learn more about how they work with different travel and tourism organisations.

'Then we worked in groups in the learning centre. Each group researched one type of organisation. Our group was responsible for travel agents, so we found out information about the different types of travel agents and made a presentation to the class. Each group did something different, so that by the end we knew a lot about different types of travel and tourism organisations.

'Finally we carried out further research on our own. I produced articles about the different types of organisations. I got a merit grade for this assignment. I might even try an upgrade to a distinction because I can see from the feedback what more I need to do to improve my work.'

Underline five different methods used by Joe and his group to find out information to complete the assignment. Which would you find the most useful?

Getting the most from your BTEC

Getting the most from your BTEC involves several skills, such as using your time effectively and working well with other people. Knowing yourself is also important.

Knowing yourself

How would you describe yourself? Make some notes here.

_____

_____

_____

_____

_____

_____

_____

_____

If you described yourself to someone else, would you be able to sum up your temperament and personality, identify your strengths and weaknesses and list your skills? If not, is it because you've never thought about it or because you honestly don't have a clue?

Learning about yourself is often called self-analysis. You may have already done personality tests or careers profiles. If not, there are many available online. However, the information you gain from these profiles is useless unless you can apply it to what you are doing.

Your personality

Everyone is different. For example, some people:
- like to plan in advance; others prefer to be spontaneous
- love being part of a group; others prefer one or two close friends
- enjoy being the life and soul of the party; others prefer to sit quietly and feel uncomfortable at large social gatherings
- are imaginative and creative; others prefer to deal only with facts
- think carefully about all their options before making a decision; others follow their 'gut instincts' and often let their heart rule their head.

Case study: Personality traits

Leah was pleased to see that a local college was offering a taster day for the BTEC First in Travel and Tourism. She had been undecided about the course, so she decided to sign up for the taster day to find out more.

During the taster day, Leah is struck by how different the participants are. There are some real extroverts who seem very confident and are always the first ones to volunteer an answer or take a lead part in an activity. There are a couple of people who are much quieter and barely speak in the group activities, although Leah finds them very friendly when talking to them during the breaks. Others, like Leah, seem somewhere in the middle – friendly but not overpowering.

The tutors give them a great introduction to travel and tourism. They explain that there is no such thing as a perfect personality for working in the sector – indeed, one of the tasks on taster day is looking at different personalities for different kinds of travel and tourism jobs.

Leah can see that there are many jobs that would suit people with *big* personalities, those who are the life and soul of the party, but there are many more jobs for those who have other qualities like being friendly, well-organised and helpful.

They carry out some group activities during the taster day and these help to show some of the personality traits of people in the group. Leah finds that she is seen as being fun, friendly and supportive, all qualities that would be sought after in the travel and tourism sector.

In what ways is your personality suited to the BTEC Travel and Tourism course you are studying?

TRY THIS

Imagine one of your friends is describing your best features. What would they say?

Personalities in the workplace

There's a mix of personalities in most workplaces. Some people prefer to work behind the scenes, such as many IT practitioners, who like to concentrate on tasks they enjoy doing. Others love high-profile jobs and being involved in high-pressure situations, such as paramedics and television presenters. Most people fall somewhere between these two extremes.

In any job there will be some aspects that are more appealing and interesting than others. If you have a part-time job you will already know this. The same thing applies to any course you take!

Your personality and your BTEC First course

Understanding your personality means you can identify which parts of your course you are likely to find easy and which more difficult. Working out the aspects you need to develop should be positive. You can also think about how your strengths and weaknesses may affect other people.

- Natural planners find it easier to schedule work for assignments.
- Extroverts like giving presentations and working with others but may overwhelm quieter team members.
- Introverts often prefer to work alone and may be excellent at researching information.

Activity: What is your personality type?

1a) Identify your own personality type, either by referring to a personality test you have done recently or by going online and doing a reliable test. Go to page 106 to find out how to access an online test.

Print a summary of the completed test or write a brief description of the results for future reference.

b) Use this information to identify the tasks and personal characteristics that you find easy or difficult.

> **BTEC FACT**
>
> All BTEC First courses enable you to develop your personal, learning and thinking skills (**PLTS**), which will help you to meet new challenges more easily. (See page 97.)

	Easy	Difficult
Being punctual		
Planning how to do a job		
Working neatly and accurately		
Being well organised		
Having good ideas		
Taking on new challenges		
Being observant		
Working with details		
Being patient		
Coping with criticism		
Dealing with customers		
Making decisions		
Keeping calm under stress		
Using your own initiative		

	Easy	Difficult
Researching facts carefully and accurately		
Solving problems		
Meeting deadlines		
Finding and correcting own errors		
Clearing up after yourself		
Helping other people		
Working as a member of a team		
Being sensitive to the needs of others		
Respecting other people's opinions		
Being tactful and discreet		
Being even-tempered		

2 Which thing from your 'difficult' list do you think you should work on improving first? Start by identifying the benefits you will gain. Then decide how to achieve your goal.

Your knowledge and skills

You already have a great deal of knowledge, as well as practical and personal skills gained at school, at home and at work (if you have a part-time job). Now you need to assess these to identify your strengths and weaknesses.

To do this accurately, try to identify evidence for your knowledge and skills. Obvious examples are:

- previous qualifications
- school reports
- occasions when you have demonstrated particular skills, such as communicating with customers or colleagues in a part-time job.

TOP TIPS

The more you understand your own personality, the easier it is to build on your strengths and compensate for your weaknesses.

Part-time jobs give you knowledge and skills in a real work setting.

Activity: Check your skills

1 Score yourself from 1 to 5 for each of the skills in the table below.

1 = I'm very good at this skill.

2 = I'm good but could improve this skill.

3 = This skill is only average and I know that I need to improve it.

4 = I'm weak at this skill and must work hard to improve it.

5 = I've never had the chance to develop this skill.

Enter the score in the column headed 'Score A' and add today's date.

2 Look back at the units and topics you will be studying for your course – you entered them into the chart on pages 9–10. Use this to identify any additional skills that you know are important for your course and add them to the table. Then score yourself for these skills, too.

3 Identify the main skills you will need in order to be successful in your chosen career, and highlight them in the table.

Go back and score yourself against each skill after three, six and nine months. That way you can monitor your progress and check where you need to take action to develop the most important skills you will need.

English and communication skills	Score A	Score B (after three months)	Score C (after six months)	Score D (after nine months)
Test dates:				
Reading and understanding different types of texts and information				
Speaking to other people face to face				
Speaking clearly on the telephone				
Listening carefully				
Writing clearly and concisely				
Presenting information in a logical order				
Summarising information				
Using correct punctuation and spelling				
Joining in a group discussion				
Expressing your own ideas and opinions appropriately				
Persuading other people to do something				
Making an oral presentation and presenting ideas clearly				
ICT skills	Score A	Score B (after three months)	Score C (after six months)	Score D (after nine months)
Test dates:				
Using ICT equipment correctly and safely				
Using a range of software				
Accurate keyboarding				
Proofreading				
Using the internet to find and select appropriate information				
Using ICT equipment to communicate and exchange information				
Producing professional documents which include tables and graphics				
Creating and interpreting spreadsheets				
Using PowerPoint				

Maths and numeracy skills	Score A	Score B (after three months)	Score C (after six months)	Score D (after nine months)
Test dates:				
Carrying out calculations (eg money, time, measurements etc) in a work-related situation				
Estimating amounts				
Understanding and interpreting data in tables, graphs, diagrams and charts				
Comparing prices and identifying best value for money				
Solving routine and non-routine work-related numerical problems				

Case study: Past experience

If you ask different people why they have chosen a travel and tourism course, it is likely that their past experiences of travelling have had something to do with their decision. Maybe when on holiday they have seen people carrying out their jobs and thought that they would like to do something like that.

Each year, for as long as she could remember, Zara had taken a holiday abroad with her family. As soon as she arrived at the overseas airport she was in her element, watching the holiday representatives in their work. Last year she had spoken to one of the reps who told her that she had taken a travel and tourism course. She suggested that Zara should consider doing the same and that she should also try to gain some customer service experience. Zara followed her advice, signed up for a course and found a part-time job working in a busy shop.

Harry felt he was something of an expert on travel because his family had a small villa in Cyprus, so they headed off to the sun at least twice a year. He loved everything about airports and airlines. He could see himself working in an airport in a really busy environment.

Ranjita had completed work experience in a travel agency. She loved watching the travel agents dealing with customers, helping them to find the holidays of their dreams. The agents looked so smart in their uniforms, and Ranjita enjoyed the whole atmosphere in the agency. It was very calm and professional and she had to play her part by looking smart, providing a welcome to customers, and keeping the brochure racks neat and tidy. She enjoyed it very much and created such a good impression that she was offered some part-time work for a few hours each Saturday.

Have you had a particular holiday or travel experience that has made you want to work in travel and tourism?

Managing your time

Some people are brilliant at managing their time. They do everything they need to and have time left over for activities they enjoy. Other people complain that they don't know where the time goes.

Which are you? If you need help to manage your time – and most people do – you will find help here.

Why time management is important

- It means you stay in control, get less stressed and don't skip important tasks.
- Some weeks will be peaceful, others will be hectic.
- The amount of homework and assignments you have to do will vary.
- As deadlines approach, time always seems to go faster.
- Some work will need to be done quickly, maybe for the next lesson; other tasks may need to be done over several days or weeks. This needs careful planning.
- You may have several assignments or tasks to complete in a short space of time.
- You want to have a social life.

Avoiding time-wasting

We can all plan to do work, and then find our plans go wrong. There may be several reasons for this. How many of the following do *you* do?

Top time-wasting activities
1 Allowing (or encouraging) people to interrupt you.
2 Not having the information, handouts or textbook you need because you've lost them or lent them to someone else.
3 Chatting to people, making calls or sending texts when you should be working.
4 Getting distracted because you simply must keep checking out MySpace, Facebook or emails.
5 Putting off jobs until they are a total nightmare, then panicking.
6 Daydreaming.
7 Making a mess of something so you have to start all over again.

Planning and getting organised

The first step in managing your time is to plan ahead and be well organised. Some people are naturally good at this. They think ahead, write down their commitments in a diary or planner, and store their notes and handouts neatly and carefully so they can find them quickly.

How good are your working habits?

Improving your planning and organisational skills

1 Use a diary or planner to schedule working times into your weekdays and weekends.

2 Have a place for everything and everything in its place.

3 Be strict with yourself when you start work. If you aren't really in the mood, set a shorter time limit and give yourself a reward when the time is up.

4 Keep a diary in which you write down exactly what work you have to do.

5 Divide up long or complex tasks into manageable chunks and put each 'chunk' in your diary with a deadline of its own.

6 Write a 'to do' list if you have several different tasks. Tick them off as you go.

7 Always allow more time than you think you need for a task.

Talking to friends can take up a lot of time.

TRY THIS

Analyse your average day.

How many hours do you spend sleeping, eating, travelling, attending school or college, working and taking part in leisure activities?

How much time is left for homework and assignments?

Case study: Getting organised

Amy is hoping to work in travel and tourism when she leaves school. Here she reflects on her organisational skills.

'It's always been something of a joke in our family that I am hopeless at organising myself. I always seem to be running around at the last minute doing my homework and getting my things ready for school. My mum has often commented that it's strange how I can organise myself when it comes to meeting friends and going out, but not when it comes to organising my school work.

'When I started my BTEC Travel and Tourism course we were told how important it was to be well organised as this would help us to keep up with deadlines. We were given planners and shown how manage our time when planning assignment work. It didn't seem too difficult to stay on top of the work, and I decided that I was going to turn over a new leaf and be more organised.

'I didn't do too badly at the start of the course. When we received our assignment schedule I entered all the dates into my planner. The first two or three tasks were fine, but then I missed one deadline, then another, and somehow things snowballed from there. Before I knew it I was so busy trying to catch up on late work that I missed more deadlines.

'My tutor advised me on how to get back on track by helping me to set up a realistic action plan to catch up and then keep up with my deadlines. I now have some set times for doing my coursework and a big message board in my room with key dates. I don't want to fall behind again because it is demotivating. By keeping up I am much more in control, and I'm also finding that I am achieving some higher grades too.'

Do you ever miss deadlines?

What steps could you take to become better organised?

TOP TIPS

If you become distracted by social networking sites or email when you're working, set yourself a time limit of 10 minutes or so to indulge yourself.

BTEC FACT

If you have serious problems that are interfering with your ability to work or to concentrate, talk to your tutor. There are many ways in which BTEC learners who have personal difficulties can be supported to help them continue with their studies.

Activity: Managing time

1 The correct term for something you do in preference to starting a particular task is a 'displacement activity'. In the workplace this includes things like often going to the water cooler to get a drink, and constantly checking emails and so on online. People who work from home may tidy up, watch television or even cook a meal to put off starting a job.

Write down *your* top three displacement activities.

2 Today is Wednesday. Sajid has several jobs to do tonight and has started well by making a 'to do' list. He's worried that he won't get through all the things on his list and, because he works on Thursday and Friday evenings, that the rest will have to wait until Saturday.

a) Look through Sajid's list and decide which jobs are top priority and *must* be done tonight and which can be left until Saturday if he runs out of time.

b) Sajid is finding that his job is starting to interfere with his ability to do his assignments. What solutions can you suggest to help him?

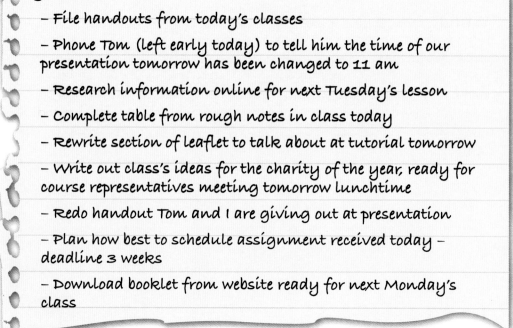

Jobs to do
- File handouts from today's classes
- Phone Tom (left early today) to tell him the time of our presentation tomorrow has been changed to 11 am
- Research information online for next Tuesday's lesson
- Complete table from rough notes in class today
- Rewrite section of leaflet to talk about at tutorial tomorrow
- Write out class's ideas for the charity of the year, ready for course representatives meeting tomorrow lunchtime
- Redo handout Tom and I are giving out at presentation
- Plan how best to schedule assignment received today – deadline 3 weeks
- Download booklet from website ready for next Monday's class

Getting the most from work experience

On some BTEC First courses, all learners have to do a **work placement**. On others, they are recommended but not essential, or are required only for some optional units. If you are doing one, you need to prepare for it so that you get the most out of it. The checklists in this section will help.

Before you go checklist

1. Find out about the organisation by researching online.

2. Check that you have all the information you'll need about the placement.

3. Check the route you will need to take and how long it will take you. Always allow longer on the first day.

4. Check with your tutor what clothes are suitable and make sure you look the part.

5. Check that you know any rules or guidelines you must follow.

6. Check that you know what to do if you have a serious problem during the placement, such as being too ill to go to work.

7. Talk to your tutor if you have any special personal concerns.

8. Read the unit(s) that relate to your placement carefully. Highlight points you need to remember or refer to regularly.

9. Read the assessment criteria that relate to the unit(s) and use these to make a list of the information and evidence you'll need to obtain.

10. Your tutor will give you an official logbook or diary – or just use a notebook. Make notes each evening while things are fresh in your mind, and keep them safely.

While you're on work placement

Ideally, on your first day you'll be told about the business and what you'll be expected to do. You may even be allocated to one particular member of staff who will be your 'mentor'. However, not all firms operate like this, and if everyone is very busy, your **induction** may be rushed. If so, stay positive and watch other people to see what they're doing. Then offer to help where you can.

BTEC FACT

If you need specific evidence from a work placement for a particular unit, your tutor may give you a logbook or work diary, and will tell you how you will be assessed in relation to the work that you will do.

TRY THIS

You're on work experience. The placement is interesting and related to the job you want to do. However, you've been watching people most of the time and want to get more involved. Identify three jobs you think you could offer to do.

While you're there

1 Arrive with a positive attitude, knowing that you are going to do your best and get the most out of your time there.

2 Although you may be nervous at first, don't let that stop you from smiling at people, saying 'hello' and telling them your name.

3 Arrive punctually – or even early – every day. If you're delayed for any reason, phone and explain. Then get there as soon as you can.

4 If you take your mobile phone, switch it off when you arrive.

5 If you have nothing to do, offer to help someone who is busy or ask if you can watch someone who is doing a job that interests you.

6 Always remember to thank people who give you information, show you something or agree that you can observe them.

7 If you're asked to do something and don't understand what to do, ask for it to be repeated. If it's complicated, write it down.

8 If a task is difficult, start it and then check back that you are doing it correctly before you go any further.

9 Obey all company rules, such as regulations and procedures relating to health and safety and using machinery, the use of IT equipment, and access to confidential information.

10 Don't rush off as fast as you can at the end of the day. Check first with your mentor or supervisor whether you can leave.

Coping with problems

Problems are rare but can happen. The most common ones are being bored because you're not given any work to do or upset because you feel someone is treating you unfairly. Normally, the best first step is to talk to your mentor at work or your supervisor. However, if you're very worried or upset, you may prefer to get in touch with your tutor instead – do it promptly.

TOP TIPS

Observing people who are skilled at what they do helps you learn a lot, and may even be part of your **assignment brief**.

Getting experience of work in travel and tourism

Although a work placement is not a compulsory part of the BTEC First in Travel and Tourism qualification, it is always a useful experience to sample working life if you have the opportunity to do so.

Getting work placements in some organisations in travel and tourism can be difficult. Most opportunities for work experience arise with travel agents, hotels, visitor attractions and tour operators. However it is much more difficult in airports and with airlines, because strict security measures mean that work experience is very rarely possible.

The choice of organisations for work placement will be largely dependent on where you live and how far you are able to travel. To help you to plan work experience in travel and tourism, you will need to follow a number of steps.

1 List here the locations (for example, towns, cities, specific areas) you can realistically reach from home using public transport to work normal daytime hours (9 am to 5 pm).

2 By using the internet and telephone directories, and by talking to your tutor or careers adviser, list the travel and tourism organisations you can find within the locations you listed in step one. If you live in an area where there is a lot of choice, then confine your search to a smaller area.

Travel agents (leisure or business travel)
Hotels
Tourist information centres
Visitor attractions
Tour operators
Transport providers, such as local coach or rail operators
Tourist providers, such as boat trips, guided bus tours
Other

3 From the lists, select your 'top ten' potential work placement providers, taking into account the type of organisation, type of work, its exact location, accessibility and travel costs.

Now it should be much easier to narrow down your choices for work placement.

When considering the type of work placement, you need to think how about particular types of organisations will provide different experiences for you. For example, a porter in a large hotel will help to carry luggage to customers' rooms, but this role also involves providing a welcome, chatting to guests, being polite and answering their questions. Here are some of the experiences you might have when working as a porter in a hotel.

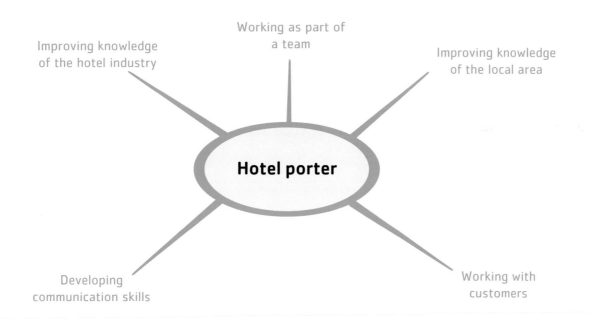

Complete a spider diagram in the space below to show the experiences you might have in a work placement of your choice, such as working in a travel agency or tourist information centre.

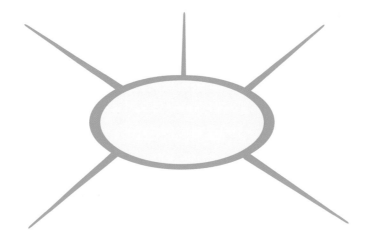

There are many benefits to completing work experience in travel and tourism, but there can be some downsides too.

Think about what are the advantages and disadvantages of work experience *for you*, by taking into account your personality and personal circumstances. Try to think of at least five advantages and five disadvantages.

Advantages eg skills development, employment	Disadvantages eg clash with part-time job, cost of transport

Advantages eg skills development, employment	Disadvantages eg clash with part-time job, cost of transport

Case study: Ana's work experience placement

Ana is in year 11 at school and has secured a work placement at Crossways independent travel agency. She had to visit the agency for an informal interview before they would confirm the placement. This is what Ana had to say about the interview:

'I was feeling a little bit nervous when I found out I had to attend an interview. I made sure I was smartly dressed and punctual. When I arrived, the manager, Ian, introduced me to the team and they all seemed very friendly. He asked me what I knew about the agency, so I was pleased that I had done a little bit of homework and knew what to say.

'Ian explained that there were certain tasks I would not be able to carry out during a work placement, but that I would be able to listen, observe, answer the telephone and learn from the staff. He asked me if I was interested in working for a travel agency, and I said that I hoped the placement would help me to decide on that.

'Ian went through what he expected of me during the placement, including time-keeping, appearance and attitude, and then he asked me what I hoped to gain from the experience. I told him about my course and how the work experience would help me to learn more about the skills used in retail travel, including customer service skills and using technology. I also hoped it would help to make me more aware of different tour operators and the range of holidays they offer.'

How could work placement with a travel agent contribute to your skills development?

Work experience observations

Work experience is an excellent way of seeing how an organisation's policies and procedures are actually carried out in practice. Take customer service for example: an organisation may have a customer charter stating its promise to its customers, but whether its staff always deliver on that promise is another matter.

Observing staff in the workplace is an excellent way of finding out how customer service is carried out, and that can provide useful information for your assignment.

Read these observations by two learners on their work experience at two different travel agencies:

Agency 1	Agency 2
When customers enter the agency, someone always acknowledges them and offers them a seat, even if all staff are busy.	Agency staff often sit in the back office chatting, and even do this when customers are waiting.
Brochure racks are always kept full; one of my roles on work experience is to keep them tidy and well stocked.	The brochure racks are restocked every Monday morning, which means that supplies are often running low by the end of the week.
Staff are treated courteously by the manager, and the atmosphere is really friendly for both customers and staff.	The manager is a battle axe and does not motivate staff. They feel negative and this is reflected in their work.
Staff take it in turn to answer the phone. Calls are only left to go to answerphone as a last resort when everyone is busy. All phone messages are responded to within two hours.	The telephone is automatically switched to the answerphone and calls are listened to twice a day.
The agency sends a 'Welcome Home' card to every customer when they return from holiday.	Staff only communicate with customers after their holiday if they come in to make a complaint.

You can tell much about an organisation's approach to customer service from these observations.

Can you see how a period of work experience could provide you with useful information for your assignments?

Working with other people

Everyone finds it easy to work with people they like and far harder with those they don't. On your course you'll often be expected to work as a team to do a task. This gives you practice in working with different people.

You will be expected to:

- contribute to the task
- listen to other people's views
- adapt to other people's ways of working
- take responsibility for your own contribution
- agree the best way to resolve any problems.

These are quite complex skills. It helps if you understand the benefits to be gained by working cooperatively with other people and know the best way to achieve this.

BTEC FACT

An important part of your BTEC course is learning how to work positively and productively with other people.

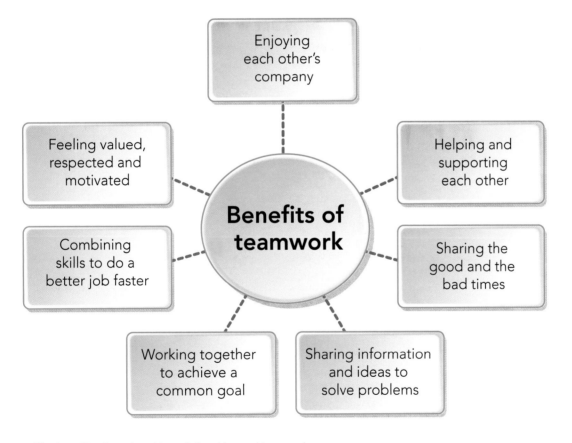

The benefits of good working relationships and teamwork.

Golden rules for everyone (including the team leader!)

The secret of a successful team is that everyone works together. The role of the team leader is to make this as easy as possible by listening to people's views and coordinating everyone's efforts. A team leader is not there to give orders.

Positive teamwork checklist
✔ Be loyal to your team, including the team leader.
✔ Be reliable and dependable at all times.
✔ Be polite. Remember to say 'please' and 'thank you'.
✔ Think before you speak.
✔ Treat everyone the same.
✔ Make allowances for individual personalities. Give people 'space' if they need it, but be ready to offer support if they ask for it.
✔ Admit mistakes and apologise if you've done something wrong – learn from it but don't dwell on it.
✔ Give praise when it's due, give help when you can and thank people who help you.
✔ Keep confidences, and any promises that you make.

Do you:

a) shrug and say nothing in case he gets upset?

b) ask why he didn't text you to give you warning?

c) say that it's the last time you'll ever go anywhere with him and walk off?

Which do you think would be the most effective – and why?

Case study: A team approach to planning a study visit

Monika and her fellow school students were excited when they were given the opportunity to put forward proposals and plans for a forthcoming study visit. They soon organised themselves informally into a team, with a willing team leader and lots of volunteers to take on other roles. A meeting was arranged to set out objectives for the trip and to decide on a plan of action.

The tutor took a back seat and allowed the group to work through the agenda it had set. However, chaos reigned at the first meeting. The agenda fell by the wayside as everyone joined in and put forward various views on how things should be done. The group ran out of time and didn't achieve much.

It was clear from this meeting that the project would never get off the ground unless some rules were put in place. The tutor arranged for the class to regroup, and asked them how they felt their initial meeting had gone. They all agreed that it had not been a success.

Under the tutor's guidance the class started again.

- They identified the different tasks involved in organising the study trip and this enabled them to create specific roles, such as researching transport and accommodation options, proposing destinations for consideration, setting a budget and giving the team leader clear responsibilities.

- They agreed a timeframe for initial tasks and timetabled regular meetings to monitor and report on progress.

- The minutes of this meeting were typed up and a copy was given to all members of the class. This clearly recorded everyone's designated roles and responsibilities, and listed action points and deadlines.

Can you see how this new approach would give the project a better chance of success?

There are many benefits to be gained from working as a team.

Activity: Golden rules

Can you imagine how disorganised the in-flight service would be if the aircraft's cabin crew did not work effectively as part of a team? Prior to take-off there is a pre-flight briefing when crew are allocated their specific roles and tasks for the flight. Clear roles and responsibilities are fundamental to providing a safe and efficient service to customers. A successful flight is then dependent on each member of the team fulfilling their own roles and responsibilities and being supportive of others.

The projects you complete as part of your BTEC First in Travel and Tourism will also depend on good teamwork. The study visit described in the case study on page 37 is a typical example of a project requiring clear lines of responsibility and clearly defined roles.

A good team leader is essential for team success. A leader needs to earn the respect of the team. This can be a difficult role in a class situation, especially if a vote has been taken to decide on the leader, and the person who wins the vote is not everyone's first choice.

Come up with three golden rules for being an effective team leader.

1

2

3

It is essential that all team members pull their weight if there is to be a good working relationship within the team. Resentment is caused when some members of the team are not as committed as others. This might happen, for example, if some members of the team disagree with the choice of destination for the study visit.

Suggest three golden rules for how you can show commitment to the team.

1

2

3

Planning is central to the success of a study visit. There are many components to organise, such as transport and accommodation. For example, there is little point in having accommodation organised if the team members planning transport haven't carried out their tasks.

Come up with three golden rules for effective planning.

1

2

3

Not everyone can take a leading role when planning a study visit. A good team needs excellent support from those involved in the day-to-day tasks, and it is essential that all members, whatever their roles, are also made to feel valued.

Come up with three golden rules for helping people to feel valued as part of the team.

1

2

3

Mutual cooperation and respect is another feature of good teamwork. Bickering and arguments are not productive; in fact, they can be counter-productive and can result in you failing to pass your assignment.

Come up with three golden rules for fostering mutual cooperation within the team.

1

2

3

Team meetings

Team meetings can be vital when preparing for a study visit. When carried out effectively, team meetings will help to ensure planning is on track and provide a framework for remedial action. Good team meetings will move the project forward. Important decisions will be made at the team meetings, such as deciding on the destination, dates and costs for the study visit.

When taking part in meetings, it is important that you express yourself clearly yet also take into consideration the views and feelings of others. Sometimes it is necessary to accept a majority decision with good grace, even when you would have preferred the decision to have gone another way.

It's not wrong to disagree with proposals, but criticism must be constructive. Can you rephrase the following comments so that they become more constructive?

What was said...	How it might have been said...
That itinerary just doesn't work. Ours is much better.	
That's a really boring trip. Who would want to pay for that?	
Why do you think you always know best?	
What do you mean you can't afford it?	

Getting the most from special events

BTEC First courses usually include several practical activities and special events. These enable you to find out information, develop your skills and knowledge in new situations and enjoy new experiences. They may include visits to external venues, visits from specialist speakers, and team events.

Industry visits give you the opportunity to see first hand how businesses operate.

Most learners enjoy the chance to do something different. You'll probably look forward to some events more than others. If you're ready to get actively involved, you'll usually gain the most benefit. It also helps to make a few preparations!

Case study: Getting the most from a visit

Alandra's group is due to visit a large hotel to find out about its policies, processes and resources for customer service.

Prior to the visit Alandra's teacher suggests that they should look at their assignment brief and design a question sheet to make sure that they get all the information they need from the visit to help them with their assignment.

Alandra has produced a template in preparation for the visit. She has organised it into three sections.

Section A

• Size and type of organisation

Section B

• Customer service policy

• Mission statement

• Complaints policy

Section C

• Numbers (and types) of staff employed

• Internal customer service, such as incentives, rewards

• Budget considerations for staff training etc

Alandra finds she can complete Section A before the visit by using the hotel's website. She is also able to view the hotel's customer service policy and its mission statement on the website.

By carrying out some of the research in advance, Alandra gains a reasonable insight into the organisation. Her research highlights areas where the visit is going to have to provide essential information for her assignment, such as the complaints policy and everything for Section C. She feels well prepared and knows how important it will be to gain first-hand knowledge from the visit in order to fill in the gaps and expand on the information she has gathered so far.

Can you see how advance preparation has helped Alandra to get the most from the visit?

Special events checklist

✔ Check you understand how the event relates to your course.

✔ If a visit or trip is not something you would normally find very interesting, try to keep an open mind. You might get a surprise!

✔ Find out what you're expected to do, and any rules or guidelines you must follow, including about your clothes or appearance.

✔ Always allow enough time to arrive five minutes early, and make sure you're never late.

✔ On an external visit, make notes on what you see and hear. This is essential if you have to write about it afterwards, use your information to answer questions in an assignment, or do something practical.

✔ If an external speaker is going to talk to your class, prepare a list of questions in advance. Nominate someone to thank the speaker afterwards. If you want to record the talk, it's polite to ask first.

✔ For a team event, you may be involved in planning and helping to allocate different team roles. You'll be expected to participate positively in any discussions, to talk for some (but not all) of the time, and perhaps to volunteer for some jobs yourself.

✔ Write up any notes you make as soon as you can – while you can still understand what you wrote!

TRY THIS

At the last minute, you're asked to propose a vote of thanks to a visiting speaker on behalf of your class. What would you say?

Activity: Meet the rep

Abi works as a holiday representative and is pleased to be asked back to her old college to meet current learners and answer questions about her job. The tutor has briefed her that the learners are looking at opportunities for employment in travel and tourism so they are particularly interested in finding out about the roles and responsibilities of her job.

Meeting people who work in the industry will provide valuable information.

Imagine that you are one of the learners who will be attending Abi's talk.

Put together three questions to find out the main roles and responsibilities of Abi's job.

1

2

3

Put together another three questions to find out about the main skills and qualities needed to be successful as a holiday rep.

1

2

3

Write another three questions designed to help you find out about the positives and negatives of the job:

1

2

3

What are the benefits of finding out this information from Abi, rather than researching using the internet?

Resources and research

Understanding resources

Resources are items that help you do something. The most obvious one is money! To obtain your BTEC First award, however, your resources are rather different.

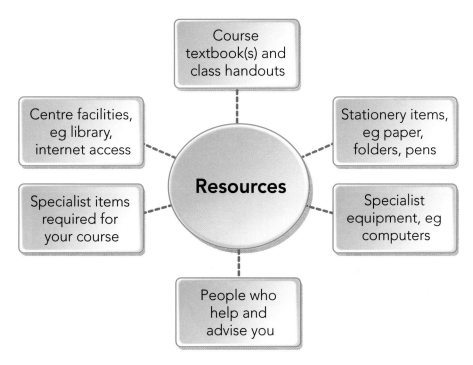

Course textbook(s) and class handouts

Centre facilities, eg library, internet access

Specialist items required for your course

Resources

Stationery items, eg paper, folders, pens

Specialist equipment, eg computers

People who help and advise you

Different kinds of resources

Physical resources

Physical resources are things like textbooks, computers and any specialist equipment.

- Popular textbooks, laptops for home use and specialist equipment may need to be booked. Leaving it until the last minute is risky.
- You can ask for help if you don't know how to use resources properly.
- You should check what stationery and equipment you need at the start of your course and make sure you have it.
- You need to look after your resources carefully. This saves money and time spent replacing lost items.

People as resources

There are many people who can help you through your course:

- family members who help and support you
- your tutor
- friends in your group who collect handouts for you and phone you to keep you up to date when you're absent
- librarians and computer technicians, at your centre or your local library
- expert practitioners.

Expert practitioners

Expert practitioners have worked hard to be successful in their chosen area. They know the skills and knowledge needed to do the job properly. They can be invaluable when you're researching information (see page 53). You can also learn a lot by watching them at work, especially if you can ask them questions about what they do, what they find hard, and any difficulties they've had.

A marketing executive must have the confidence and expertise to give presentations to large or small groups of colleagues.

Try to observe more than one expert practitioner:

- It gives you a better picture about what they do.
- No single job will cover all aspects of work that might apply to your studies.
- You may find some experts more approachable and easy to understand than others. For example, if someone is impatient because they're busy it may be difficult to ask them questions, or if someone works very quickly you may find it hard to follow what they're doing.

If you have problems, just note what you've learned and compare it with your other observations. And there's always the chance that you're observing someone who's not very good at their job! You'll only know this for certain if you've seen what people should be doing.

Activity: Create your own resource list

Being out and about on holiday and trips is one of the best ways of experiencing travel and tourism products and services. However, to develop your knowledge of the sector and to understand how different organisations work together, you will need to use several resources.

- **Textbooks**

  There are several textbooks that have been written specifically to support the BTEC First in Travel and Tourism. These cover the units you are studying, and their contents form the basis of what you will need to learn. You will also find that the textbooks contain useful activities that you can complete in your own time to further develop your knowledge and understanding.

- **Newspapers and magazines**

  Many newspapers (particularly the weekend editions) and magazines have travel supplements containing interesting features on different types of holidays. There are often articles on new, adventurous or unusual types of holidays, and the advertisements usually promote travel and tourism products and services. The specialist 'trade' newspapers can be useful for finding out what is going on in the sector. Your school or college might subscribe to these trade publications.

- **Television**

  Some 'fly-on-the-wall' documentary television programmes follow the day-to-day work in airports or holiday destinations. These can give an excellent insight into work in different types of organisations. They are well worth watching. Holiday channels can introduce you to many destinations and different types of holidays.

- **Internet**

  The internet opens up the world of travel at the press of a button. You can use it to find out about destinations and to plan journeys, as well as to book holidays, accommodation, transport and tickets to attractions. Most travel and tourism organisations have their own websites where you can take virtual tours of hotels, attractions and holiday destinations. Google Earth is an excellent resource for helping you to see where destinations are located.

- **People**

  People can be one of your best resources when finding out about customer service, or carrying out research into destinations. It is useful to draw on people's travel experiences – good and bad – so talk to friends and relatives about what they liked about holidays, hotels, attractions and other travel and tourism services, and what they disliked.

- **Holiday brochures**

  Holiday brochures are another excellent resource, but they are expensive for tour operators to produce so you should not go into travel agencies and pick up lots of brochures to help you with your assignments. However, if you go to your local travel agency and ask the manager, you may find that the agency is willing to let you have copies of brochures that are no longer needed.

- **Maps and atlases**

  Althugh many excellent resources are now available on the internet, being able to use maps and atlases effectively is a skill that is still highly valued in the travel and tourism sector. In addition to maps, the *Columbus World Travel Atlas* contains useful information that will help you with assignments.

- **Guidebooks**

  There are many excellent guidebooks available if you wish to read up about specific destinations. Most libraries have a wide selection of guidebooks that you can use for research.

- **Stationery**

  You should always make sure you are equipped with pens and pencils, along with a file to keep handouts, notes and work you complete for homework tasks. A small notebook might also be useful for making notes when undertaking visits.

Create a resource list using the grid below. Look at the suggested resources in the unit specifications to help you.

Library-based resources – eg textbooks, newspapers and magazines, maps and atlases, guidebooks
Internet-based resources – eg websites
People and businesses – eg relatives and friends, travel agents for holiday brochures
Stationery

Finding the information you need

The information explosion

There are lots of different ways to find out information – newspapers, magazines, books, television, radio, CDs, DVDs, the internet. And you can exchange information with other people by texting, sending an email or phoning someone.

All this makes it much easier to obtain information. If you know what you're doing, you can probably find most of what you need sitting at a computer. But there are some dangers:

- Finding exactly what you want online takes skill. You need to know what you're doing.
- It's easy to get too much information and become overwhelmed.
- It's unlikely that everything you need will be available online.
- The information you read may be out of date.
- The information may be neither reliable nor true.

> Define what you are trying to find. (The more precise you are, the more likely you are to find what you're looking for.)

> Know where to look for it. (Remember: the internet is not the only source of information.)

> Recognise when you have found appropriate information.

> Know what to do with information once you've found it. (Make sure that you understand it, interpret it correctly and record the source where you found it.)

> Know when to stop looking (especially if you have a deadline).

Finding and using information effectively

Before you start

There are four things that will help you look in the right place and target your search properly.

Ask yourself ...	Because ...	Example
Exactly what do I need to find out?	It will save you time and effort.	If you need information about accidents, you need to know what type of accident and over what time period.
Why do I need this information and who is going to read it?	This puts the task into context. You need to identify the best type of information to obtain and how to get it.	If you're making a poster or leaflet for children, you'll need simple information that can be presented in a graphical format. If, however, you're giving a workplace presentation on accidents, you'll need tables and graphs to illustrate your talk.
Where can I find it?	You need to consider whether your source is trustworthy and up to date. The internet is great, but you must check that the sites you use are reliable.	To find out about accidents in the workplace you could talk to the health and safety at work officer. To find examples of accidents in your local area you could look through back copies of your local newspaper in the local library or newspaper offices.
What is my deadline?	You know how long you have to find the information and use it.	

Your three main sources of information are:
- libraries or learning resource centres
- the internet
- asking other people, for example through interviews and questionnaires.

Researching in libraries

You can use the learning resource centre in your school or college, or a local public library. Public libraries usually have a large reference section with many resources available for loan, including CD-ROMs, encyclopaedias, government statistics, magazines, journals and newspapers, and databases such as Infotrac, which contains articles from newspapers and magazines over the last five years.

The librarian will show you how to find the resources you need and how to look up a specific book (or author) to check if it is available or is out on loan.

Some books and resources can only be used in the library itself, while others can be taken out on short-term or long-term loan. You need to plan how to access and use the resources that are popular or restricted.

Using your library

✔ If your centre has an intranet you might be able to check which books and CD-ROMs are available without actually visiting the library.

✔ All libraries have photocopying facilities, so take enough change with you to copy articles that you can't remove. Write down the source of any article you photocopy, ie the name and the date of the publication.

✔ Learn how to keep a reference file (or bibliography) in which you store the details of all your sources and references. A bibliography must include CDs, DVDs and other information formats, not just books and magazines.

✔ If your search is complicated, go at a quiet time when the librarian can help you.

✔ Don't get carried away if you find several books that contain the information you need. Too many can be confusing.

✔ Use the index to find information quickly by searching for key words. Scan the index using several likely alternatives.

✔ Only use books that you find easy to understand. A book is only helpful if you can retell the information in your own words.

Researching online

A good search engine such as Google will help you find useful websites. They look for sites based on the information you enter in the search box. In some cases, such as Ask.co.uk, you may get the chance to refine your choice after entering your key words or question.

Finding information on a website

Wikipedia is a popular free online encyclopaedia. It has been criticised because entries may be inaccurate, as members of the public can edit the site. However, Wikipedia is trying to prevent this by organising professional editing.

If you're not sure whether something you read is correct, or if there is anything strange about it, check it against information on another site. Make sure you ask your tutor's opinion, too.

With large websites, it can be difficult to find what you need. Always read the whole screen – there may be several menus in different parts of the screen.

To help you search, many large websites have:
- their own search facility or a site map that lists site content with links to the different pages
- links to similar sites where you might find more information. Clicking a link should open a new window, so you'll still be connected to the original site.

TRY THIS

Search engines don't just find websites. On Google, the options at the top of your screen include 'images', 'news' and 'maps'. If you click on 'more' and then 'even more', you'll find other options, too. You'll usually find the most relevant information if you use the UK version of a search engine. Only search the whole web if you deliberately want to include European and American information. Go to page 106 to find out how you can see this in action.

There may be useful information and links at the top, foot or either side of a web page.

There are several other useful sites you could visit when researching online.

- **Directory sites** show websites in specific categories so you can focus your search at the start.

- **Forums** are sites, or areas of a website, where people post comments on an issue. They can be useful if you want to find out opinions on a topic. You can usually read them without registering.

- **News sites** include the BBC website as well as the sites for all the daily newspapers. Check the website of your local newspaper, too.

Printing information

- Only print information that you're sure will be useful. It's easy to print too much and find yourself drowning in paper.

- Make quick notes on your print-outs so that you remember why you wanted them. It will jog your memory when you're sorting through them later.

- If there's a printer-friendly option, use it. It will give you a print-out without unnecessary graphics or adverts.

- Check the bottom line of your print-outs. It should show the URL for that page of the website, and the date. You need those if you have to list your sources or if you want to quote from the page.

TRY THIS

Go to page 106 to find out how to access a website where you can see how directory sites work.

TOP TIPS

Bookmark sites you use regularly by adding the URL to your browser. How to do this will depend on which browser you use, eg Internet Explorer, Firefox.

Researching by asking other people

You're likely to do this for two reasons:
- you need help from someone who knows a lot about a topic
- you need to find out several people's opinions on something.

Information from an expert

Explain politely why you are carrying out the investigation. Ask questions slowly and clearly about what they do and how they do it. If they don't mind, you could take written notes so you remember what they tell you. Put the name and title of the person, and the date, at the top. This is especially important if you might be seeing more than one person, to avoid getting your notes muddled up.

Ask whether you may contact them again, in case there's anything you need to check. Write down their phone number or email address. Above all, remember to say 'thank you'!

The opinions of several people

The easiest way to do this is with a questionnaire. You can either give people the questionnaire to complete themselves, or interview them and complete it yourself. Professional interviewers often telephone people to ask questions, but at this stage it's not a good idea unless you know the people you're phoning and they're happy for you to do this.

Whether you've found lots of information or only a little, assessing what you have and using it wisely is very important. This section will help you avoid the main pitfalls.

Devising a questionnaire

1 Make sure it has a title and clear instructions.

2 Rather than ask for opinions, give people options, eg yes/no, maybe/always, never/sometimes. This will make it easier to analyse the results.

3 Or you can ask interviewees to give a score, say out of 5, making it clear what each number represents, eg 5 = excellent, 4 = very good.

4 Keep your questionnaire short so that your interviewees don't lose interest. Between 10 and 15 questions is probably about right, as long as that's enough to find out all you need.

5 Remember to add 'thank you' at the end.

6 Decide upon the representative sample of people you will approach. These are the people whose views are the most relevant to the topic you're investigating.

7 Decide how many responses you need to get a valid answer. This means that the answer is representative of the wider population. For example, if you want views on food in your canteen, it's pointless only asking five people. You might pick the only five people who detest (or love) the food it serves.

TOP TIPS

Design your questionnaire so that you get quantifiable answers. This means you can easily add them up to get your final result.

TRY THIS

Always test your draft questionnaire on several people, to highlight any confusing questions or instructions.

Case study: Designing questionnaires

Jacob is investigating UK destinations as part of his BTEC First in Travel and Tourism. A visit to Blackpool has been organised in order to find out about the appeal of the destination.

Before the visit Jacob and his classmates carried out some research on the internet, so he already had a good idea of what Blackpool has to offer. However, their tutor advised them that they must identify the appeal for a specific type of visitor. Jacob and his group have to find out about the appeal of Blackpool for retired people.

They find it difficult to imagine Blackpool through the eyes of a retired person, so they decided to put together a questionnaire and to carry out some research. They used the unit specification to help them design a questionnaire. They wrote questions to find out what attracted retired people to Blackpool, including:

- visitor attractions
- beach/coast
- shopping
- accommodation
- facilities, such as shops and restaurants
- sightseeing
- events, theatres etc
- transport – coach and train services to Blackpool, local buses, trams etc.

Jacob and his friends carried out the survey using retired family members and neighbours. They pooled all their responses and this gave them a good idea of what attracted retired people to Blackpool. When they actually visited Blackpool they were much better prepared to see the resort through the eyes of a retired person.

Other members of the class adopted a similar approach for different visitor types, such as families, teenagers and school groups. Each group made a presentation on the appeal of Blackpool for their visitor type, giving the class an excellent insight into how Blackpool attracts different types of visitors.

How could research using other people benefit you in other units?

Activity: Research

Some units require you to keep evidence of different sources of information you have used. For example, for Unit 6: UK Tourism Destinations you have to 'be able to use sources of information to find out about UK destinations'.

You have to provide evidence that you have used both paper-based and online resources. These could include guidebooks, tourist leaflets, atlases and holiday brochures.

It is a good idea to keep a record of the resources you have used as you go along. Your record should:

- list the resources you used and the materials you looked at
- state full website URLs where appropriate
- sum up very briefly the appropriateness of each resource.

Below is an extract from the research log of Ben, who is investigating
Blackpool as a UK seaside destination.

Name: Ben Freeman

Assignment: The appeal of UK destinations

Source/material	When and where found	Brief summary of information gathered	Comments
Internet – Blackpool website	www.visitblackpool.com 5 Feb	Attractions, events, accommodation, transport	Excellent – official website Good coverage of all aspects for assignment
Daily Express	Travel supplement 5 Feb	Detailed article on Blackpool as a special interest destination	Includes some new attractions and gives a different insight into Blackpool

Use the blank log below to find and record some sources that you could use
to find out information about Blackpool as a UK seaside destination.

Source/material	When and where found	Brief summary of information gathered	Comments

Keeping a logbook

For some units, such as Unit 13: Organising a Travel and Tourism Study Visit, a logbook can be used to record the preparations being made for the visit. This is your personal record of your involvement in the arrangements. If you are involved in making arrangements for the transport, it should provide a record of all your communications with transport companies, including a brief summary of telephone calls, copies of emails and so on.

If you are required to keep a logbook, make sure that you complete it regularly when the work you have undertaken is still fresh in your mind.

Below is an example from a process log produced by a learner involved in planning for a study visit as a part of her BTEC First in Travel and Tourism.

Karina Baker Process log – Thursday 3rd December
Summary of work undertaken so far
Last week we finalised the destination. It is definitely going to be a trip to Blackpool, taking place during the first week in April for four days. I have to obtain quotes for transport and report back at the next meeting on 10 December.
Actions carried out today
I researched on the internet and obtained the contact details for four local coach companies. I met with the transport subgroup and we decided that we should ask for quotes for a 50-seater coach, both with and without WC to see if there is much difference in cost. I sent an email to four coach companies to ask them for a quote for a four-day trip starting on either 2 or 3 April. The coach will take us to and from Blackpool, and stay with us during the visit to transport us around the resort.
What needs to be done next?
Chase the quotes before the next meeting.

Why is it important for Karina to record her actions in this way?

Why is it important to keep the log up to date?

Managing your information

Whether you've found lots of information or only a little, assessing what you have and using it wisely is very important. This section will help you avoid the main pitfalls.

Organising and selecting your information

Organising your information

The first step is to organise your information so that it's easy to use.
- Make sure your written notes are neat and have a clear heading – it's often useful to date them, too.
- Note useful pages in any books or magazines you have borrowed.
- Highlight relevant parts of any handouts or leaflets.
- Work out the results of any questionnaires you've used.

Selecting your information

Re-read the **assignment brief** or instructions you were given to remind yourself of the exact wording of the question(s) and divide your information into three groups:
1 Information that is totally relevant.
2 Information that is not as good, but could come in useful.
3 Information that doesn't match the questions or assignment brief very much but that you kept because you couldn't find anything better!

Check there are no obvious gaps in your information against the questions or assignment brief. If there are, make a note of them so that you know exactly what you still have to find. Although it's ideal to have everything you need before you start work, don't delay if you're short of time.

Putting your information in order

Putting your information in a logical order means you can find what you want easily. It will save you time in the long run. This is doubly important if you have lots of information and will be doing the work over several sessions.

Case study: Ed's scrapbook

'Travel and tourism is a fast-moving sector, and it is often affected by events around the world. Our tutor suggested that we keep a scrapbook of useful articles that we come across as this would be a good resource for future assignment work, especially for Unit 4: Development of the UK Travel and Tourism Sector.

'I have divided my file into four sections:

- economic, such as articles on the collapse of airlines, failure of tour operators, oil price rises, changing currency exchange rates
- political, such as political unrest, outbreaks of war, terrorism
- environmental, such as climate change, natural disasters, pandemics
- social, such as unemployment, recession

'I have found that there is something in the newspapers most weeks. I hadn't imagined that so many things in the news would have such an impact on the travel and tourism sector. I am finding it very interesting to work out the links. For example, when I had read about the poor value of the pound against the euro I hadn't really thought about how that would put people off travelling to Europe and how it would also make it more expensive to contract hotels.

'Also I am very concerned about the environment and I am interested to see what travel and tourism organisations are doing to be more environmentally responsible. I have been quite impressed with the policies of several well-known organisations.

'I am pleased that our teacher suggested that we build up a scrapbook, because I have found many useful articles and photographs and I feel very well prepared for my assignment work.'

How could building a scrapbook help you in other units?

Activity: Producing templates

In many assignments for your BTEC First in Travel and Tourism you will have cover a fair amount of content. The assignment briefs will list what needs to be addressed. It is important to check that you are covering everything that is required, and a good way to make sure you don't miss anything out is to produce a template on the computer.

For example, in Unit 6: UK Tourism Destinations, to meet grading criterion P2 you need to describe the appeal of one UK town or city destination, one seaside resort and one countryside area, each focusing on appeal for a different type of visitor. So you need to produce content for three destinations. By producing three templates for suitable destinations, you will see at a glance what needs to be addressed, and this will help to focus your research. Notes can be typed directly into the expandable boxes and then extended into a description when sufficient information has been found. The box lines can be hidden so that the printed work flows better.

CITY: York
Visitor attractions: such as the National Trust, English Heritage, theme parks, museums, historical sites, heritage sites, wildlife parks
Natural features: such as mountains, beaches, lakes, rivers, coast
Range of accommodation: such as hotels, guesthouses, B&B, self-catering, camping and caravanning, holiday parks, boats
Facilities: such as sport and leisure facilities, shopping
Arts and entertainment: such as theatres, art galleries, exhibitions, festivals and events

Sightseeing: such as guided tours, ghost walks, boat trips, road trips, trains
Transport links: such as different types of transport to York and transport options in the city

If you have addressed the right amount of content, you will be well on the way to achieving the pass criteria.

Produce your own template to organise material for presentations in a similar format.

Interpreting and presenting your information

The next stage is to use your information to prepare the document and/or oral presentation you have to give. There are four steps:

1 Understand what you're reading.

2 Interpret what you're reading.

3 Know the best form in which to produce the information, bearing in mind the purpose for which it is required.

4 Create the required document so that it's in a suitable layout with correct spelling and punctuation.

Understanding what you read

As a general rule, never use information that you don't understand. However, nobody understands complex or unfamiliar material the first time they read it, especially if they just scan through it quickly. Before you reject it, try this:

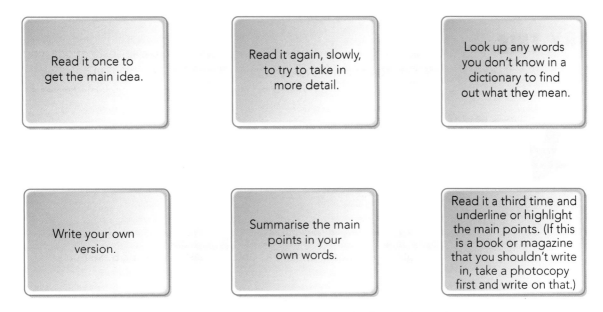

Read it once to get the main idea.

Read it again, slowly, to try to take in more detail.

Look up any words you don't know in a dictionary to find out what they mean.

Write your own version.

Summarise the main points in your own words.

Read it a third time and underline or highlight the main points. (If this is a book or magazine that you shouldn't write in, take a photocopy first and write on that.)

Special note: Show both the article and your own version to your tutor to check your understanding. This will help you identify any points you missed out and help you improve your skills of interpreting and summarising.

Understanding unfamiliar information

Interpreting what you read

Interpreting what you read is different from understanding it. This is because you can't always take it for granted that something you read means what it says. The writer may have had a very strong or biased opinion, or may have exaggerated for effect. This doesn't mean that you can't use the information.

Strong opinions and bias

People often have strong points of view about certain topics. This may be based on reliable facts, but not always! We can all jump to conclusions that may not be very logical, especially if we feel strongly about something.

Things aren't always what they seem to be. Are these boys fighting or are they having a good time?

Exaggeration

Many newspapers exaggerate facts to startle and attract their readers.

LOCAL FIRM DOUBLES STAFF IN TWO WEEKS!

This newspaper headline sounds very positive. You could easily think it means employment is growing and there are more jobs in your area. Then you read on, and find the firm had only four staff and now has eight!

Tables and graphs

You need to be able to interpret what the figures mean, especially when you look at differences between columns or rows. For example, your friend might have an impressive spreadsheet that lists his income and expenditure. In reality, it doesn't tell you much until you add the figures up and subtract one from the other. Only then can you say whether he is getting into debt. And even if he is, you need to see his budget over a few months, rather than just one which may be exceptional.

Choosing a format

You may have been given specific instructions about the format and layout of a document you have to produce, in which case life is easy as long as you follow them! If not, think carefully about the best way to set out your information so that it is clear.

Different formats	Example
text	when you write in paragraphs or prepare a report or summary
graphical	a diagram, graph or chart
pictorial	a drawing, photograph, cartoon or pictogram
tabular	numerical information in a table

The best method(s) will depend on the information you have, the source(s) of your material and the purpose of the document – a leaflet for schoolchildren needs graphics and pictures to make it lively, whereas a report to company shareholders would be mainly in text form with just one or two graphs.

Stating your sources

Whatever format you use, if you are including other people's views, comments or opinions, or copying a table or diagram from another publication, you must state the source by including the name of the author or publication, or the web address. This can be in the text or as part of a list at the end. Failure to do this (so you are really pretending other people's work is your own) is known as **plagiarism**. It is a serious offence with penalties to match.

TOP TIPS

Never make assumptions or jump to conclusions. Make sure you have all the evidence to support your views.

TOP TIPS

Don't just rely on your spellchecker. It won't find a word spelled wrongly that makes another valid word (eg from/form), so you must proofread everything. And remember to check whether it is set to check American English or British English. There are some spelling differences.

Text format

Creating written documents gets easier with practice. These points should help.

Golden rules for written documents

1 Think about who will be reading it, then write in an appropriate language and style.

2 Ensure it is technically correct, ie no wrong spellings or bad punctuation.

3 Take time to make it look good, with clear headings, consistent spacing and plenty of white space.

4 Write in paragraphs, each with a different theme. Leave a line space between each one.

5 If you have a lot of separate points to mention, use bullets or numbered points. Numbered points show a certain order or quantity (step 1, step 2 etc). Use bullet points when there is no suggested order.

6 Only use words that you understand the meaning of, or it might look as if you don't know what you mean.

7 Structure your document so that it has a beginning, middle and end.

8 Prepare a draft and ask your tutor to confirm you are on the right track and are using your information in the best way.

Graphical format

TRY THIS ➡

Someone asks for directions to your house. Would you write a list or draw a diagram? Which would be easier for you and for the other person – and why?

Most people find graphics better than a long description for creating a quick picture in the viewer's mind. There are several types of graphical format, and you can easily produce any of these if you have good ICT skills.

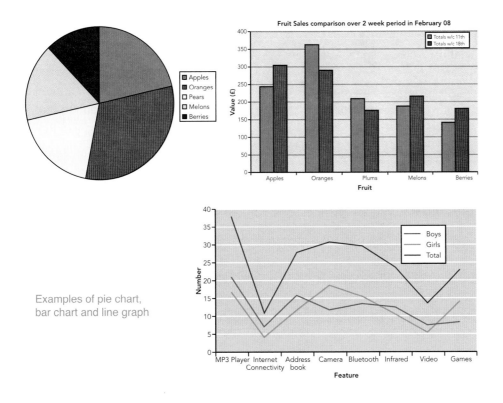

Examples of pie chart, bar chart and line graph

Pictorial format

Newspapers and magazines use pictures to illustrate situations and reduce the number of words needed. It doesn't always have to be photographs though. For example, a new building may be sketched to show what it will look like.

A pictogram or pictograph is another type of pictorial format, such as charts which use the image of an object (fruit, coins, even pizzas) to represent data, such as the number eaten or amount spent.

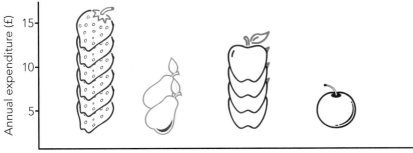

TOP TIPS

Don't spend hours writing text when an illustration can do the job better – but make sure the illustration you choose is suitable for the document and the reader.

Tabular format

A table can be an easy way to communicate information. Imagine a retailer preparing information about the items in stock. Text would be difficult to understand and comparisons between stock levels and sales would be almost impossible to make. A table, however, would easily show the fastest-selling items.

Tables are also ideal if you are showing rankings – such as best-selling music or books.

Bestsellers list – September 2009

Position	Title	Author	Imprint	Publication
1 (New)	Lost Symbol,The	Brown, Dan	Bantam Press	15-Sep-2009
2 (1)	Complaints, The	Rankin, Ian	Orion	03-Sep-2009
3 (New)	Return Journey, The	Binchy, Maeve	Orion	17-Sep-2009
4 (7)	Sapphire	Price, Katie	Century	30-Jul-2009
5 (9)	Wolf Hall	Mantel, Hilary	Fourth Estate	30-Apr-2009
6 (3)	Week in December, A	Faulks, Sebastian	Hutchinson	03-Sep-2009
7 (2)	Alex Cross's Trial	Patterson, James	Century	10-Sep-2009
8 (4)	White Queen, The	Gregory, Philippa	Simon & Schuster Ltd	18-Aug-2009
9 (5)	Even Money	Francis, Dick & Francis, Felix	Michael Joseph	03-Sep-2009
10 (8)	206 Bones	Reichs, Kathy	William Heinemann	27-Aug-2009

National newspaper circulation – September 2009

	August 2009	August 2008	% change on last year	August 09 (without bulks)	March 2009 – August 2009	% change on last year
Sun	3,128,501	3,148,792	-0.64	3,128,501	3,052,480	-2.25
Daily Mail	2,171,686	2,258,843	-3.86	2,044,079	2,178,462	-4.45
Daily Mirror	1,324,883	1,455,270	-8.96	1,324,883	1,331,108	9.44
Daily Star	886,814	751,494	18.01	886,814	855,511	16.65
The Daily Telegraph	814,087	860,298	-5.37	722,644	807,328	-6.73
Daily Express	730,234	748,664	-2.46	730,234	727,824	-1.32
Times	576,185	612,779	-5.97	529,746	588,471	-4.63
Financial Times	395,845	417,570	-5.2	365,269	411,098	-6.7
Daily Record	347,302	390,197	-10.99	345,277	350,306	-10.59
Guardian	311,387	332,587	-6.37	311,387	332,790	-4.11
Independent	187,837	230,033	-18.34	148,551	198,445	-16.76

Activity: Presenting information

Your BTEC in Travel and Tourism will require you to present information for several reasons. The table below gives some examples (in the first column) of information you might need to present during your course.

For each example, what type of format do you think would be best for presenting the information? Choose from:

- text format
- graphical format (including spidergrams)
- pictorial format
- tabular format.

Type of information	Format
The results of a customer survey about satisfaction with service in a hotel	
Information gathered about the development of the travel and tourism sector	
Information about cash flow and profits	
The results of an audit of the visitor numbers to a visitor attraction – with data on the sales of adult tickets, family tickets, concessions*	
Ideas for an advertisement for a new travel and tourism service	
A review of sunshine and temperatures in a destination	
A list of the types of organisations that can be found in travel and tourism and how they relate to one another	
Information about the number of tickets sold for three performances of an event, including full price tickets and concessions*.	

*Tickets sold at a reduced price for particular groups of people, such as children, students or retired people.

Making presentations

Presentations help you to learn communication skills.

Some people hate the idea of standing up to speak in front of an audience. This is quite normal, and you can use the extra energy from nerves to improve your performance.

Presentations aren't some form of torture devised by your tutor! They are included in your course because they help you learn many skills, such as speaking in public and preparing visual aids. They also help you practise working as a team member and give you a practical reason for researching information. And it can be far more enjoyable to talk about what you've found out rather than write about it!

There's a knack to preparing and giving a presentation so that you use your energies well, don't waste time, don't fall out with everyone around you and keep your stress levels as low as possible. Think about the task in three stages: preparation, organisation and delivery.

Preparation

TOP TIPS

Keep visual aids simple but effective, and check any handouts carefully before you make lots of copies.

Start your initial preparations as soon as you can. Putting them off will only cause problems later. Discuss the task in your team so that everyone is clear about what has to be done and how long you have to do it in.

Divide any research fairly among the team, allowing for people's strengths and weaknesses. You'll also need to agree:

- which visual aids would be best
- which handouts you need and who should prepare them
- where and when the presentation will be held, and what you should wear
- what questions you might be asked, both individually and as a team, and how you should prepare for them.

Once you've decided all this, carry out the tasks you've been allocated to the best of your ability and by the deadline agreed.

Organisation

This is about the planning you need to do as a team so that everything will run smoothly on the day.

Delivery

This refers to your performance during the presentation. Being well prepared and well organised helps stop you panicking. If you're very nervous at the start, take a few deep breaths and concentrate on the task, not yourself. It's quite normal to be nervous at the start but this usually fades once you get under way. You might even enjoy it …

Top tips for delivering a good presentation

✔ Rehearse, rehearse, rehearse!

✔ Write notes on flash cards to remind you of key things that you need to say.

✔ Practise looking up from your cards when you are talking.

✔ Time yourself to see if your presentation lasts for the time allocated.

✔ Include illustrations and slides, if possible, to engage the audience.

✔ Practise saying any complicated words again and again so that they don't cause any problems in your actual presentation.

✔ Make sure you understand what you are saying – you may have questions on your presentation at the end.

What else do you think you could do to help you prepare for a presentation?

1

2

3

4

5

TOP TIPS

Never read from prepared prompt cards! Look at the audience when you're talking and smile occasionally. If you need to use prompt cards as a reminder, write clearly so that you need only glance at them.

TOP TIPS

Remember, the audience always makes allowances for some nerves!

Case study: Overcoming presentation nerves

It has become quite common for presentations to form part of the interview process for a job in the travel and tourism sector. So any presentation skills developed on the course will be useful for your future progression.

Gina doesn't like making presentations at all. She feels very nervous and speaks so quickly that people have difficulty taking in what she has to say. She has a presentation coming up for the worldwide destination unit, and her tutor is trying to develop Gina's (and her classmates') presentation skills.

Having carried out research into their chosen destinations, the tutor starts by getting each person in the class to interview another learner. The interviewer must find out what the other learner likes about the chosen destination and then present this destination to the rest of the group, explaining why it has been chosen. This is a positive start as the activity goes well and everyone does a good job. It seems to have calmed a few nerves.

The tutor then works with each learner to make sure

they have enough research information available to cover the assessment requirements for their own presentation. In most cases, learners have too much information. So the tutor instructs learners to cut out the 'padding' and he advises them to remove any big words that they might not normally use.

Once this has been done, they produce PowerPoint slides, trying to incorporate good photographs and using just a few bullet points per slide. The tutor asks everyone to inject at least one humorous or memorable fact into their presentation.

The presentations are now starting to take shape, and it's time to practise at home in front of the mirror. Cue cards are written to help with any memory loss.

When the day of the presentation comes the learners sail through, achieving just the right balance of facts and humour. The learners are all hugely supportive of one another, and it turns out to be a positive experience.

Can you think of other ways to overcome presentation nerves?

Activity: Preparation, organisation, delivery

Advance preparation is particularly important when a presentation forms part of an assignment. This is because not only will you be assessed on this activity but you will also have an audience to face. This can be daunting at the best of times, especially if you are not well prepared.

Imagine that you have to deliver a presentation for Unit 4: Development of the UK Travel and Tourism Sector. Consider how you would feel in these situations and write down how you could have been better prepared.

1 You have carried out plenty of research, but most of it has been completed at the last minute. It's now two hours before you are due to give your presentation. You have forgotten to book a computer in the learning centre so you are unable to produce a PowerPoint presentation.

2 You are due to make a group presentation and one of the members of your group has not turned up. He has the copy of your presentation slides saved on a memory stick. Nobody else in the group has a copy.

3 You have just finished your presentation on the development of travel and tourism sector and someone asks you a question that you cannot answer.

4 You are working as part of a group to deliver a presentation on the development of the travel and tourism sector, but you are arguing about who is going to deliver each part of the presentation.

Case study: Learner quotes about making presentations

Most people start off feeling uncomfortable about talking in front of a group of people, whether you know them or not. This is what some real learners have said about having to give presentations as part of their BTEC course.

'I actually feel more comfortable giving a presentation rather than having to write an essay. What I really enjoy about it is the fact that sometimes we have to prepare a presentation as a whole group. I like that we work together to find information and then we take turns presenting different points. The fact that I am not the only one out there and I am part of a supportive team makes it fun for me.'

Gabriela, 16, BTEC Level 2 First in Performing Arts

'Although presentations are very stressful, when I present my work it helps to hang my ideas together and I find I can express what I want to say more clearly than when I write things down. Instant feedback is helpful and boosts my confidence for the next time.'

Ethan, 19, BTEC Level 2 First in Creative Media Production

'I think presentations are useful but I find them difficult to deliver – relying heavily on my memory, which is very nerve-wracking. We were told that presentation would be part of our assessment. I really worried about it and couldn't sleep the night before – stressing out about what I was going to say. I hated the first few minutes, but after that I was OK.'

Will, 16, BTEC Level 2 First in Engineering

'I was very nervous about presenting to my class until I took part in the Young Enterprise scheme and had to present the results of our project to over 200 people, including the mayor! After that presenting to my classmates didn't feel too nerve-wracking at all.'

Lizzy, 17, BTEC Level 2 First in Business

'I used to dread presentations on my course, but found that if I went through my notes again and again until I knew the presentation inside out, it made it much easier, and the presentations generally went well.'

Javinder, 17, BTEC Level 3 National in Construction

'I used to hate presenting to other people on my course, until I realised that most of them were as nervous about it as I was!'

Koichi, 21, BTEC Level 3 National in Art and Design

'Less is more! I used to rely on props and, as I was nervous about forgetting things or running out of things to say, I talked far too quickly. I had to repeat everything as nobody knew what I was on about! Some of my best presentations have been done without using slides or any other props at all, just talking (slowly of course) to my audience.'

Laura, 18, BTEC Level 3 National in Health & Social Care

'I used to be petrified of talking in front of other people but over time I've learned that, if I prepare well before a presentation, I usually feel much more confident on the day. If I know my material, I don't have to look down at my notes all the time and can make eye contact with the audience. Taking a few deep breaths before I begin keeps me calm and allows me to focus.'

Katie, 19, BTEC Level 3 National in Creative Media Production

'I prefer to be assessed by oral presentations as I'm dyslexic and my written work lets me down all the time. Everyone tells me that I really shine and show that I know my stuff when I present it to the rest of the group.'

Sam, 17, BTEC Level 3 National in Business

Your assessments

The importance of assignments

All learners on BTEC First courses are assessed by means of **assignments**. Each one is designed to link to specific **learning outcomes** and **grading criteria**. At the end of the course, your assignment grades put together determine your overall grade.

To get the best grade you can, you need to know the golden rules that apply to all assignments, then how to interpret the specific instructions.

10 golden rules for assignments

1   Check that you understand the instructions.

2   Check whether you have to do all the work on your own, or if you will do some as a member of a group. If you work as a team, you need to identify which parts are your own contributions.

3   Always write down any verbal instructions you are given.

4   Check the final deadline and any penalties for not meeting it.

5   Make sure you know what to do if you have a serious personal problem, eg illness, and need an official extension.

6   Copying someone else's work (**plagiarism**) is a serious offence and is easy for experienced tutors to spot. It's never worth the risk.

7   Schedule enough time for finding out the information and doing initial planning.

8   Allow plenty of time between talking to your tutor about your plans, preparations and drafts, and the final deadline.

9   Don't panic if the assignment seems long or complicated. Break it down into small, manageable chunks.

10   If you suddenly get stuck, ask your tutor to talk things through with you.

Case study: Assignment feedback

Eryl has just got feedback for his market research assignment for the marketing unit on my BTEC First in Travel and Tourism.

'I enjoyed this assignment because it was an opportunity to apply theory to practical tasks. It was for Unit 10: Exploring Marketing in Travel and Tourism, and it gave us the opportunity to achieve P3, P4, M2, and D1. The feedback I have been given is very detailed and tells me exactly what I have achieved and what I need to do to achieve the higher grades.

'For P3 we had to use secondary research to meet specific objectives. My objectives were to find out about the types of visitors to Blackpool and their motivations for travelling to this resort. I was able to find some secondary research published by the tourist board to help me to achieve P3.

'For P4 I had to design and then undertake some primary research, and evaluate the results. This task was linked to P3, and I designed a questionnaire to carry out some

market research on visitors to Blackpool. The questionnaire looked pretty good, and I carried out the research when we visited Blackpool. I produced a written evaluation of the research activity.

'For M2 I had to explain how my questionnaire was appropriate and would meet the specific objectives of the research. To do this, I went through each of the questions in turn and explained what information they gave. I also explained why I had chosen a questionnaire rather than another method of research.

'I have been awarded P3, P4 and M2 for my assignment and I have received clear feedback explaining what I need to do to gain D1. I have not achieved this because I have not drawn conclusions from the research or made recommendations. I aim to complete this, as I enjoy marketing and I hope to achieve a distinction for this unit.'

Do you have the motivation to attempt the higher grades for your qualification?

Interpreting the instructions

Most assignments start with a **command word** – describe, explain, evaluate etc. These words relate to how complex the answer should be.

Command words

Learners often don't do their best because they read the command words but don't understand exactly what they have to do. These tables show you what is required for each grade when you see a particular command word.

Command words and obtaining a pass

Complete ...	Complete a form, diagram or drawing.
Demonstrate ...	Show that you can do a particular activity.
Describe ...	Give a clear, straightforward description that includes all the main points.
Identify ...	Give all the basic facts relating to a certain topic.
List ...	Write a list of the main items (not sentences).
Name ...	State the proper terms related to a drawing or diagram.
Outline ...	Give all the main points, but without going into too much detail.
State ...	Point out or list the main features.

Examples:
- **List** the main features on your mobile phone.
- **Describe** the best way to greet a customer.
- **Outline** the procedures you follow to keep your computer system secure.

Command words and obtaining a merit

Analyse ...	Identify the factors that apply, and state how these are linked and how each of them relates to the topic.
Comment on ...	Give your own opinions or views.
Compare ... Contrast ...	Identify the main factors relating to two or more items and point out the similarities and differences.
Competently use ...	Take full account of information and feedback you have obtained to review or improve an activity.
Demonstrate ...	Prove you can carry out a more complex activity.
Describe ...	Give a full description, including details of all the relevant features.
Explain ...	Give logical reasons to support your views.
Justify ...	Give reasons for the points you are making so that the reader knows what you're thinking.
Suggest ...	Give your own ideas or thoughts.

TRY THIS

Check the command word you are likely to see for each of your units in the **grading grid** in advance. This tells you the **grading criteria** for the unit so that you know the evidence you will have to present.

Examples:
- **Explain** why mobile phones are so popular.
- **Describe** the needs of four different types of customers.
- **Suggest** the type of procedures your employer would need to introduce to keep the IT system secure.

Command words and obtaining a distinction

Analyse ...	Identify several relevant factors, show how they are linked, and explain the importance of each.
Compare ... Contrast ...	Identify the main factors in two or more situations, then explain the similarities and differences, and in some cases say which is best and why.
Demonstrate ...	Prove that you can carry out a complex activity, taking into account information you have obtained or received to adapt your original idea.
Describe ...	Give a comprehensive description which tells a story to the reader and shows that you can apply your knowledge and information correctly.
Evaluate ...	Bring together all your information and make a judgement on the importance or success of something.
Explain ...	Provide full details and reasons to support the arguments you are making.
Justify ...	Give full reasons or evidence to support your opinion.
Recommend ...	Weigh up all the evidence to come to a conclusion, with reasons, about what would be best.

TOP TIPS

Think of assignments as an opportunity to demonstrate what you've learned and to get useful feedback on your work.

Examples:
- **Evaluate** the features and performance of your mobile phone.
- **Analyse** the role of customer service in contributing to an organisation's success.
- **Justify** the main features on the website of a large, successful organisation of your choice.

Getting the best result

Ask your tutor for a copy of the specification for one of the units that you are studying. Any unit will do because they are all presented in the same format. Have a look through the different sections.
- The learning outcomes state exactly what you should know, understand and be able to do when you have finished the unit.
- The unit content is the subject-specific material that you will be studying.
- The grading grid tells you what you have to present as evidence for assessment.
- There are three grading criteria: pass, merit and distinction.

Now read through the headings under the greyed-out section of the grading criteria grid. What does it say about achieving pass, merit or distinction grade? Write a brief explanation here:

Pass

Merit

Distinction

You must achieve all the pass criteria to be awarded the pass grade. You must achieve all the pass criteria and all the merit criteria to be awarded the merit grade, and you must achieve all the grading criteria to be awarded the distinction grade.

Suppose it is the end of the year, and your tutor is signing off a portfolio using a tracking sheet. This table shows a learner's performance for Unit 1: Fitness Testing and Training.

Grading criterion	P1	P2	P3	P4	P5	P6	M1	M2	M3	D1	D2
Achieved	✔	✔	✔	✔	✔	✔	✔		✔	✔	✔

This learner would be awarded a pass grade. The learner cannot be awarded a merit because M2 has not been achieved, and cannot be awarded distinction because although the learner has achieved all the distinction criteria he hasn't achieved all the grading criteria.

The grading grids use several key words and phrases. Make sure that you know what they mean.

Word/phrase	What it means
Interpret	
Analyse	
Describe	
Explain	
Evaluate	
Carry out	

With the exception of the mathematics unit, the word 'evaluate' is only ever used in the merit and distinction criteria. Use a dictionary to find a general definition for the word.

Evaluate: _____

Activity: Assignment criteria

John's class has been working on Unit 8: Worldwide Holiday Destinations. They are producing displays showing factors that impact on worldwide travel.

The pass criterion requires learners to:
- describe factors that impact on travel to worldwide destinations, giving relevant examples.

The merit criterion asks them to:
- explain how different factors impact on travel to a selected worldwide destination.

To achieve the distinction criterion they must:
- assess the impact of two factors on travel to worldwide destinations within the last five years.

John has produced an informative display. He has produced written descriptions of different factors that impact on travel, and he has included photographs to give his display visual appeal.

There is a separate display focusing on Bangkok, and this explains some of the recent issues that have affected travel to the city, including the 2009 riots. John has also produced two handouts on 'the impact of the economy on worldwide travel' and 'the impact of terrorism on worldwide travel'.

Jess has produced written description of factors that affect travel to worldwide destinations and has explained in general terms what these impacts are.

Fiona has produced detailed descriptions on a beautifully produced display board and has produced a handout entitled 'The factors that affect travel to Cuba'.

- Who appears to be on target to achieve a distinction for this part of the unit?

- Who appears to be on target to achieve a merit for this part of the unit?

- Who is likely to achieve a pass for this part of the unit?

Being assessed for practical activities

Not all of your assignments are based on your knowledge and understanding of aspects of travel and tourism. Sometimes you will have to show you are able to carry out practical activities, such as handling a complaint, dealing with an enquiry or using selling skills.

You will find that the grading grids use words to show how these practical skills will be assessed and to highlight differences between pass, merit and distinction. Usually the higher level will be determined by factors such as confidence, accuracy and independence.

Here are some of the words that appear in the grading grids for BTEC Firsts in Travel and Tourism. What do you think they mean?

○ Confidently

○ Independently

○ Efficiently

○ Coherently

○ Accurately

○ Showing creativity

○ Showing originality

○ Consistently

Sample assignment

Note about assignments
All learners are different and will approach their assignment in different ways.
The sample assignment that follows shows how one learner answered a brief to achieve pass, merit and distinction level criteria. The learner work shows just one way in which grading criteria can be evidenced. There are no standard or set answers. If you produce the required evidence for each task, then you will achieve the grading criteria covered by the assignment.

Front sheet

Add your name, date and signature to this front sheet before submitting work.

Add the completion date to your planning diary and leave plenty of time to meet the deadline.

Follow your centre's policy on how to submit your work.

Read your assignment brief carefully to see what types of evidence you are being asked to produce.

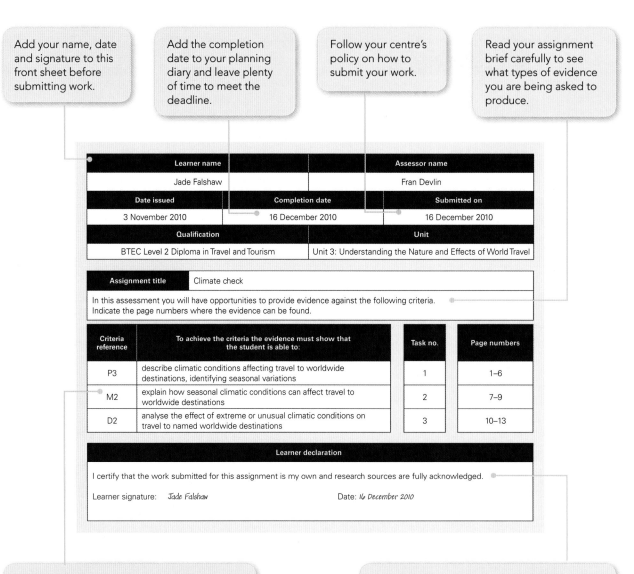

Learner name			Assessor name	
Jade Falshaw			Fran Devlin	
Date issued	**Completion date**		**Submitted on**	
3 November 2010	16 December 2010		16 December 2010	
Qualification		**Unit**		
BTEC Level 2 Diploma in Travel and Tourism		Unit 3: Understanding the Nature and Effects of World Travel		

Assignment title	Climate check

In this assessment you will have opportunities to provide evidence against the following criteria. Indicate the page numbers where the evidence can be found.

Criteria reference	To achieve the criteria the evidence must show that the student is able to:	Task no.	Page numbers
P3	describe climatic conditions affecting travel to worldwide destinations, identifying seasonal variations	1	1–6
M2	explain how seasonal climatic conditions can affect travel to worldwide destinations	2	7–9
D2	analyse the effect of extreme or unusual climatic conditions on travel to named worldwide destinations	3	10–13

Learner declaration

I certify that the work submitted for this assignment is my own and research sources are fully acknowledged.

Learner signature: *Jade Falshaw*   Date: *16 December 2010*

These are the criteria that you could achieve by completing this assignment.

You must not copy from other people, or copy extracts from books, the internet or any other sources. Your teacher will explain how to reference sources in your work.

Assignment brief

The scenario puts you into a realistic travel and tourism role and sets the scene for tasks you will carry out in this role.

This is an overview of why you are carrying out this assignment.

To 'describe' means to write clearly in full sentences to provide information on the listed topics.

Unit title	Unit 3: Understanding the Nature and Effects of World Travel
Qualification	BTEC Level 2 Diploma in Travel and Tourism
Start date	3 November 2010
Deadline date	16 December 2010
Assessor	Fran Devlin

Assignment title	Climate check

The purpose of this assignment is to:
demonstrate your knowledge of climatic conditions affecting travel to worldwide destinations.

Scenario
You are working as a trainee travel consultant with Far and Away Travel. Each month there is a staff training and briefing session when members of staff take turns to brief their colleagues on travel-related topics.

Task 1
You have been asked by your manager to make a presentation to your colleagues at the next training and briefing session. You have been asked to research and make a presentation on climatic conditions and their effect on travel to worldwide destinations. You must describe:
- at least four different climatic conditions – these can be unusual or extreme
- how these conditions can affect travel to worldwide destinations – this could be positive in attracting people to an area or negative when the conditions are extreme
- seasonal variations, including locations and times of the year to avoid, and locations and times of the year with favourable conditions.

Include global aspects in your descriptions where applicable (for example, indicate if the destination is close to the Equator or the tropics and whether it is in the northern or southern hemisphere).

Use PowerPoint software to prepare handouts for your colleagues. Keep all your notes in case your manager has any questions and make sure you reference all sources used.

This provides evidence for P3

Task 2
Your manager has asked you to also produce information sheets for your colleagues to explain climatic conditions in two destinations of your choice. Make sure that they have different climatic conditions.

In these sheets you should explain how seasonal climatic conditions can affect travel to the two destinations. For example, the climate might have a positive effect at certain times of the year, but a negative effect at other times. You could include potential effects, such as reduced or increased visitor numbers, restricted seasons, adverse publicity and potential disruption to travel plans.

This provides evidence for M2

Task 3
Many of Far and Away Travel's customers book holidays to the Caribbean. Your manager now wants you to complete more in-depth research and to produce a report on the effect of major hurricanes on the Caribbean. You can address the Caribbean in general or focus on one or more islands or destinations for your research. Your report must be analytical and you should use information from press reports, articles and other sources to support your analysis, with specific examples from within the last ten years. Identify several relevant effects, show how they are linked to travel to the Caribbean, and explain the importance of each effect.

This provides evidence for D2

These are the methods you will use to provide evidence for this assignment.

'Analytical' means that you must identify key effects, show how they are linked and explain their importance and relevance.

To 'explain' you must provide details and give reasons and evidence to support the points you are making.

These are some resources you might find useful. You must reference these and other sources used in your work.

Sources of information

Boniface, B. and Cooper, C. (2004) *Worldwide Destinations: Geography of Travel and Tourism* Butterworth-Heinemann, ISBN 0750659971

World Travel Atlas, Tenth edition (2006) Columbus Publishing, ISBN 1902221931

Websites

Foreign and Commonwealth Office www.fco.gov.uk

Columbus World Travel Guide www.worldtravelguide.net

Online atlas www.multimap.com

Met Office www.metoffice.gov.uk/education

This brief has been verified as being fit for purpose			
Assessor	Fran Devlin		
Signature	Fran Devlin	Date	1 September 2010
Internal verifier	Dan Whittle		
Signature	Dan Whittle	Date	1 September 2010

Sample learner work

This includes your name and states clearly which assignment the work relates to.

This confirms the four climatic conditions that have been selected for the task.

References to global aspects have been made.

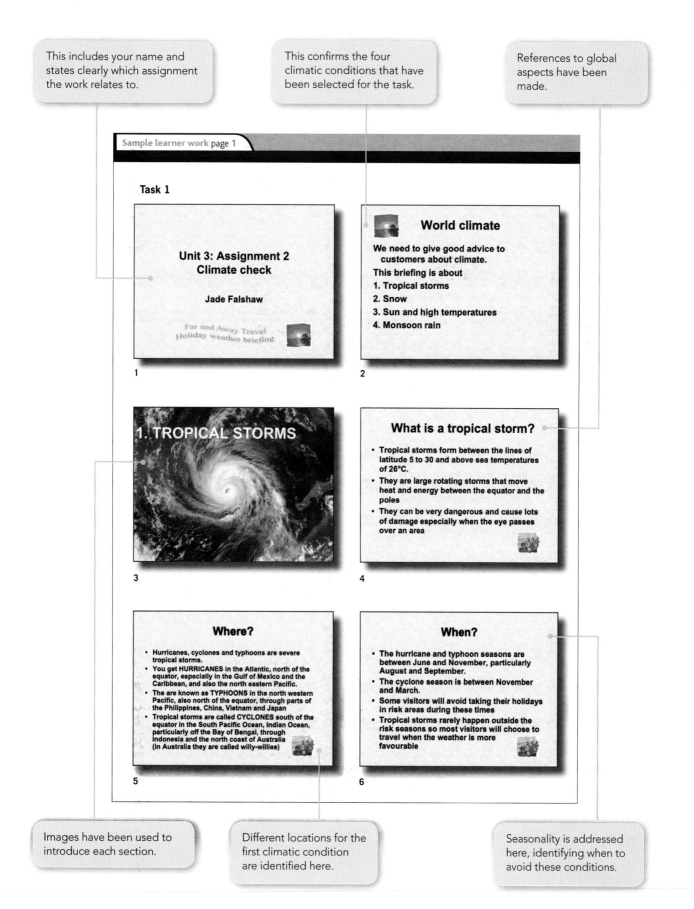

Sample learner work page 1

Task 1

**Unit 3: Assignment 2
Climate check**

Jade Falshaw

Far and Away Travel
Holiday weather briefing

1

World climate

We need to give good advice to customers about climate.

This briefing is about

1. Tropical storms
2. Snow
3. Sun and high temperatures
4. Monsoon rain

2

1. TROPICAL STORMS

3

What is a tropical storm?

- Tropical storms form between the lines of latitude 5 to 30 and above sea temperatures of 26°C.
- They are large rotating storms that move heat and energy between the equator and the poles
- They can be very dangerous and cause lots of damage especially when the eye passes over an area

4

Where?

- Hurricanes, cyclones and typhoons are severe tropical storms.
- You get HURRICANES in the Atlantic, north of the equator, especially in the Gulf of Mexico and the Caribbean, and also the north eastern Pacific.
- The are known as TYPHOONS in the north western Pacific, also north of the equator, through parts of the Philippines, China, Vietnam and Japan
- Tropical storms are called CYCLONES south of the equator in the South Pacific Ocean, Indian Ocean, particularly off the Bay of Bengal, through Indonesia and the north coast of Australia (in Australia they are called willy-willies)

5

When?

- The hurricane and typhoon seasons are between June and November, particularly August and September.
- The cyclone season is between November and March.
- Some visitors will avoid taking their holidays in risk areas during these times
- Tropical storms rarely happen outside the risk seasons so most visitors will choose to travel when the weather is more favourable

6

Images have been used to introduce each section.

Different locations for the first climatic condition are identified here.

Seasonality is addressed here, identifying when to avoid these conditions.

These are references to how travel can be affected by the first climatic condition.

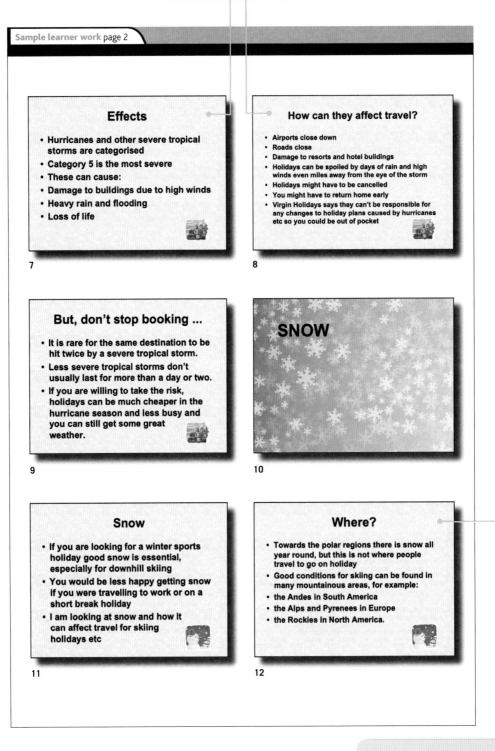

Sample learner work page 2

Effects

- Hurricanes and other severe tropical storms are categorised
- Category 5 is the most severe
- These can cause:
- Damage to buildings due to high winds
- Heavy rain and flooding
- Loss of life

7

How can they affect travel?

- Airports close down
- Roads close
- Damage to resorts and hotel buildings
- Holidays can be spoiled by days of rain and high winds even miles away from the eye of the storm
- Holidays might have to be cancelled
- You might have to return home early
- Virgin Holidays says they can't be responsible for any changes to holiday plans caused by hurricanes etc so you could be out of pocket

8

But, don't stop booking ...

- It is rare for the same destination to be hit twice by a severe tropical storm.
- Less severe tropical storms don't usually last for more than a day or two.
- If you are willing to take the risk, holidays can be much cheaper in the hurricane season and less busy and you can still get some great weather.

9

SNOW

10

Snow

- If you are looking for a winter sports holiday good snow is essential, especially for downhill skiing
- You would be less happy getting snow if you were travelling to work or on a short break holiday
- I am looking at snow and how it can affect travel for skiing holidays etc

11

Where?

- Towards the polar regions there is snow all year round, but this is not where people travel to go on holiday
- Good conditions for skiing can be found in many mountainous areas, for example:
- the Andes in South America
- the Alps and Pyrenees in Europe
- the Rockies in North America.

12

Examples of different locations for the second climatic condition are identified here, including global aspects.

Seasonality is addressed here.

Further examples of locations for the second climatic condition are shown here.

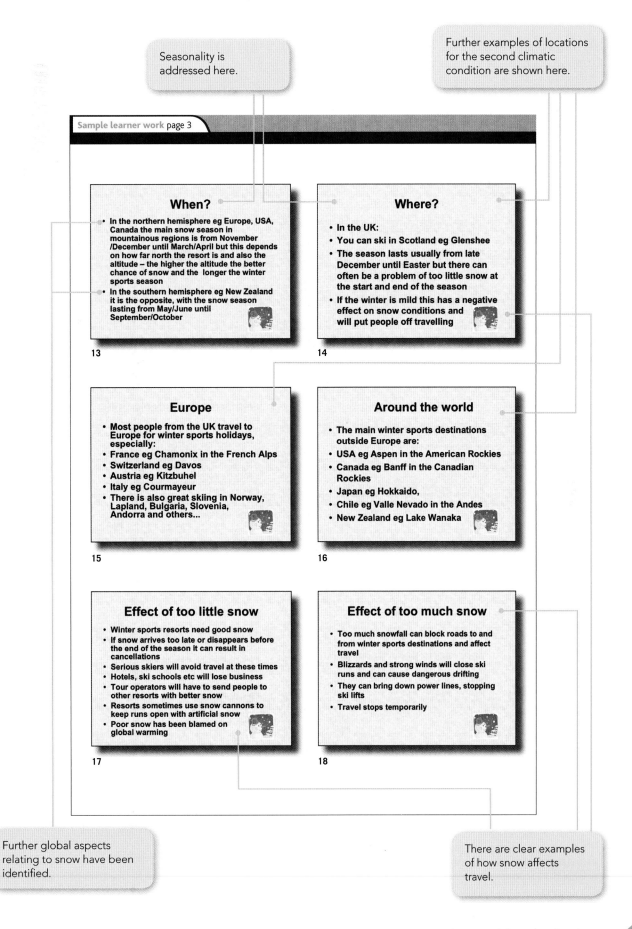

Sample learner work page 3

When?

- In the northern hemisphere eg Europe, USA, Canada the main snow season in mountainous regions is from November /December until March/April but this depends on how far north the resort is and also the altitude – the higher the altitude the better chance of snow and the longer the winter sports season
- In the southern hemisphere eg New Zealand it is the opposite, with the snow season lasting from May/June until September/October

13

Where?

- In the UK:
- You can ski in Scotland eg Glenshee
- The season lasts usually from late December until Easter but there can often be a problem of too little snow at the start and end of the season
- If the winter is mild this has a negative effect on snow conditions and will put people off travelling

14

Europe

- Most people from the UK travel to Europe for winter sports holidays, especially:
- France eg Chamonix in the French Alps
- Switzerland eg Davos
- Austria eg Kitzbuhel
- Italy eg Courmayeur
- There is also great skiing in Norway, Lapland, Bulgaria, Slovenia, Andorra and others...

15

Around the world

- The main winter sports destinations outside Europe are:
- USA eg Aspen in the American Rockies
- Canada eg Banff in the Canadian Rockies
- Japan eg Hokkaido,
- Chile eg Valle Nevado in the Andes
- New Zealand eg Lake Wanaka

16

Effect of too little snow

- Winter sports resorts need good snow
- If snow arrives too late or disappears before the end of the season it can result in cancellations
- Serious skiers will avoid travel at these times
- Hotels, ski schools etc will lose business
- Tour operators will have to send people to other resorts with better snow
- Resorts sometimes use snow cannons to keep runs open with artificial snow
- Poor snow has been blamed on global warming

17

Effect of too much snow

- Too much snowfall can block roads to and from winter sports destinations and affect travel
- Blizzards and strong winds will close ski runs and can cause dangerous drifting
- They can bring down power lines, stopping ski lifts
- Travel stops temporarily

18

Further global aspects relating to snow have been identified.

There are clear examples of how snow affects travel.

Further examples of seasonality are addressed here, inked to different locations.

Examples of seasonality and locations are provided for the third climatic condition.

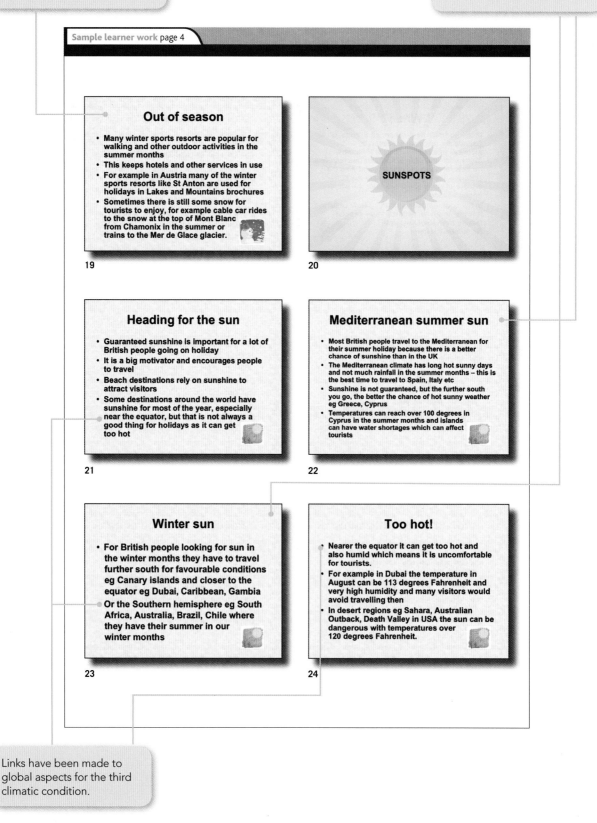

Sample learner work page 4

Out of season

- Many winter sports resorts are popular for walking and other outdoor activities in the summer months
- This keeps hotels and other services in use
- For example in Austria many of the winter sports resorts like St Anton are used for holidays in Lakes and Mountains brochures
- Sometimes there is still some snow for tourists to enjoy, for example cable car rides to the snow at the top of Mont Blanc from Chamonix in the summer or trains to the Mer de Glace glacier.

19

SUNSPOTS

20

Heading for the sun

- Guaranteed sunshine is important for a lot of British people going on holiday
- It is a big motivator and encourages people to travel
- Beach destinations rely on sunshine to attract visitors
- Some destinations around the world have sunshine for most of the year, especially near the equator, but that is not always a good thing for holidays as it can get too hot

21

Mediterranean summer sun

- Most British people travel to the Mediterranean for their summer holiday because there is a better chance of sunshine than in the UK
- The Mediterranean climate has long hot sunny days and not much rainfall in the summer months – this is the best time to travel to Spain, Italy etc
- Sunshine is not guaranteed, but the further south you go, the better the chance of hot sunny weather eg Greece, Cyprus
- Temperatures can reach over 100 degrees in Cyprus in the summer months and islands can have water shortages which can affect tourists

22

Winter sun

- For British people looking for sun in the winter months they have to travel further south for favourable conditions eg Canary islands and closer to the equator eg Dubai, Caribbean, Gambia
- Or the Southern hemisphere eg South Africa, Australia, Brazil, Chile where they have their summer in our winter months

23

Too hot!

- Nearer the equator it can get too hot and also humid which means it is uncomfortable for tourists.
- For example in Dubai the temperature in August can be 113 degrees Fahrenheit and very high humidity and many visitors would avoid travelling then
- In desert regions eg Sahara, Australian Outback, Death Valley in USA the sun can be dangerous with temperatures over 120 degrees Fahrenheit.

24

Links have been made to global aspects for the third climatic condition.

Here are some brief references to how sun affects travel, linked to named examples of destinations.

Sample learner work page 5

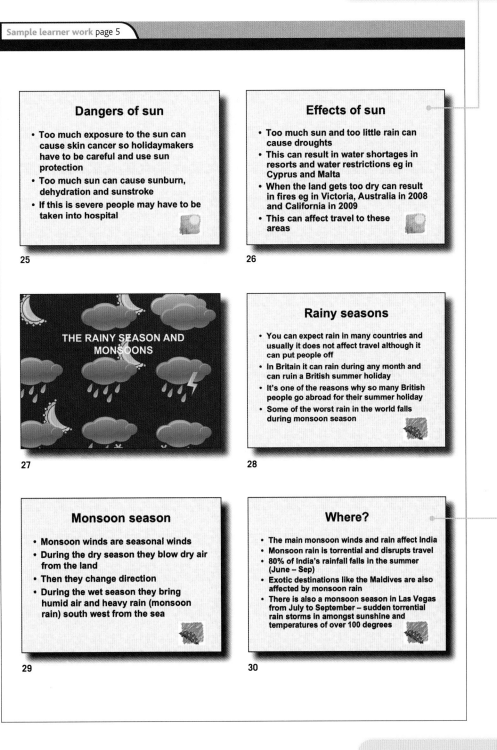

Dangers of sun

- Too much exposure to the sun can cause skin cancer so holidaymakers have to be careful and use sun protection
- Too much sun can cause sunburn, dehydration and sunstroke
- If this is severe people may have to be taken into hospital

25

Effects of sun

- Too much sun and too little rain can cause droughts
- This can result in water shortages in resorts and water restrictions eg in Cyprus and Malta
- When the land gets too dry can result in fires eg in Victoria, Australia in 2008 and California in 2009
- This can affect travel to these areas

26

THE RAINY SEASON AND MONSOONS

27

Rainy seasons

- You can expect rain in many countries and usually it does not affect travel although it can put people off
- In Britain it can rain during any month and can ruin a British summer holiday
- It's one of the reasons why so many British people go abroad for their summer holiday
- Some of the worst rain in the world falls during monsoon season

28

Monsoon season

- Monsoon winds are seasonal winds
- During the dry season they blow dry air from the land
- Then they change direction
- During the wet season they bring humid air and heavy rain (monsoon rain) south west from the sea

29

Where?

- The main monsoon winds and rain affect India
- Monsoon rain is torrential and disrupts travel
- 80% of India's rainfall falls in the summer (June – Sep)
- Exotic destinations like the Maldives are also affected by monsoon rain
- There is also a monsoon season in Las Vegas from July to September – sudden torrential rain storms in amongst sunshine and temperatures of over 100 degrees

30

Examples of seasonality and locations are provided for the fourth climatic condition.

Some of the potential effects of monsoon rains are given.

A clear list of sources has been supplied to show books and websites used in the research.

Sample learner work page 6

Effect

- Monsoon rains can cause flash floods – these can block roads
- Or major floods which can destroy buildings and cause loss of life
- Sometimes the monsoon rains don't come and this causes drought and disease
- Both of these can affect travel
- Holidaymakers may avoid travel during the monsoon season, particularly to places like the Maldives where there is nothing else to do if the weather is bad

31

Summary

- When suggesting areas for holidays, check out the typical weather for the time of the year
- Point out the risks eg hurricane season, start and end of ski seasons, monsoon season, rainfall and sunshine/humidity figures to try and help people make the best choice

32

Thank you for listening

Any questions ?

33

Sources

- www.aberdeenshire.gov.uk/sport/skicentres/glensheesk
- www.crystal.co.uk
- www.newzealand.com
- www.pacificislandtravel.com
- www.worldtravels.com
- www.metoffice.gov.uk/corporate/pressoffice/hurricanes/
- www. fco.gov.uk
- Columbus World Travel Atlas

- Images from Clipart

34

This is a good way to end a presentation – provides an opportunity to clarify any points or address any missing topics.

The task being addressed is clearly identified. For clarity, M2 could have been indicated.

The first destination selected for the task is clearly shown.

Task 2

What you need to know about climate in the Dominican Republic

The Dominican Republic is in the Caribbean and has an 'endless summer' because the temperature averages around 77 degrees Fahrenheit all year round. The Dominican Republic has seen visitor numbers increase to 4.1 million visitors in 2007, an increase of 2 per cent over 2006 figures. In 2007 it was named the 'Caribbean's Number One destination' by the World Travel Organisation. It's a real sunshine destination so it's great for beach holidays as you can see:

	Monthly high	Monthly low
January	82.0° F	70.0° F
February	82.0° F	70.0° F
March	83.0° F	71.0° F
April	84.0° F	73.0° F
May	84.0° F	75.0° F
June	86.0° F	76.0° F
July	86.0° F	76.0° F
August	86.0° F	76.0° F
September	86.0° F	75.0° F
October	86.0° F	75.0° F
November	85.0° F	73.0° F
December	82.0° F	71.0° F
Annual	**84.0° F**	**73.0° F**

Source: www.dominicanrepublic-guide.info

The best time to visit the Dominican Republic is from December to April, The weather is a bit cooler but still over 70 degrees and it is less humid. Inland and in the mountains it can get very cool (even snow on the mountain tops) but the weather can be perfect for a beach holiday. This is a great time for British people to visit the Dominican Republic so they can escape the cold in the UK.

June to October are the hottest months (up to 86 degrees Fahrenheit) but this is also when there is high humidity so it can feel very sticky as well as hot so it is not very comfortable. This is also when the main rain falls – usually in short heavy showers so that can put people off travelling there.

Another reason why some people might not want to travel to the Dominican Republic during the summer months is that June to November is the hurricane season. The worst months are August and September as can be seen in the table below:

Differences in climate at different times of the year are clearly explained, highlighting the best times to travel.

Evidence taken from websites is clearly referenced in the work.

Potential effects on travel have been identified and clearly explained.

Sample learner work page 8

| Month | Rainfall | | | % Days with | |
	Average (inches)	Max (inches)	Min (inches)	Rain	Tropical storm
January	2.2	7.6	0.2	28.2	1.0
February	1.7	5.7	0.1	30.4	2.0
March	1.9	7.9	N.A.	26.9	2.0
April	3.0	12.8	0.2	27.6	4.0
May	7.0	29.3	0.6	37.8	23.0
June	6.1	20.1	0.9	24.7	28.0
July	6.1	16.7	2.7	25.3	43.0
August	6.4	14.1	0.9	26.7	50.0
September	6.8	23.3	1.4	30.6	52.0
October	6.5	13.5	1.2	33.3	40.0
November	4.4	16.4	N.A.	32.7	18.0
December	2.5	9.2	0.2	33.4	3.0
Annual	**54.5**	**79.8**	**34.0**	**29.8**	**23.0**

Source: www. dominicanrepublic-guide.info

The last big storms to hit the Dominican Republic were Hurricane Wilma and Tropical storm Alpha in 2005 and Hurricanes Noel and Dean in 2007. These caused some disruption to travel, major flooding, structural damage and loss of life but most of this was away from the tourist areas. However there is some tropical storm activity most years and this can cause some days of bad stormy weather which people want to avoid on holiday.

The effect of the climatic conditions is that the Dominican Republic has two main seasons. The high season is in the winter months when people want to have guaranteed sunshine without the risk of hurricanes and heavy rainfall. Because demand is high the hoteliers put the prices up higher during these months. This is when the hotels are busiest and you have to book months in advance. This can make the Dominican Republic too expensive for some people.

The Dominican Republic relies on tourism to provide jobs and income. The hurricane season is the 'low season' and prices can be reduced by half to try and encourage people to travel so it is possible to get a bargain, especially during August and September, the main risk months. Many people will book late deals at this time because hurricanes can be tracked and they wait to see what the risk will be.

Sources:
www.dominicanrepublic-guide
www.fco.gov.uk
www.dominicantoday.com
www.euromonitor.com/Travel_And_Tourism_in_Dominican_Republic
www.godominicanrepublic.com

A clear list of sources has been supplied to show websites used in the research.

Positive conditions have been identified and explained.

The second destination selected for the task is clearly shown.

Sample learner work page 9

What you need to know about climate in Whistler

Whistler is one of the most popular ski resorts in British Colombia, Canada. It attracts 2.1 million overnight and non-overnight visitors each year (approximately 48 per cent in winter and 52 per cent in summer).

In 2010 it was the Host Mountain Resort for the Olympic and Paralympic Winter Games. It is part of the Coast Mountain Range and has reliable snow conditions. The average daily temperature is 22 degrees Fahrenheit during most of the winter months and daytime temperatures rarely fall below minus 10 degrees Fahrenheit. The average snowfall is over 10 metres each year and this makes it an excellent destination to travel to for winter sports.

The winter climate is quite mild because it is close to the coast, but the cool winds from the Pacific help to make the mountain snow last as long as May. The ski and snowboarding season can start as early as November. This long season makes Whistler a popular destination. The 2007–8 snow conditions were so good that the season lasted from November until early June.

There can sometimes be poor snow conditions, like the start of the 2008 snow season, but Whistler now has a 1.8 mile Peak to Peak gondola ride which means that there are more opportunities to ski at high altitude and poor snow is not so much of a problem. Snow blasters are in place to create runs for the 25 November opening if there isn't enough real snow. Fog can sometimes be a problem, especially at the beginning of the season if the weather is quite mild and this means that visibility is poor. However Whistler doesn't get the rain that affects the popularity of Vancouver.

Access to Whistler from Vancouver airport via the Sea to Sky highway can often be affected by flash snow storms. Occasionally there are massive drops in temperature, to minus 22 degrees Celsius, and very dry air, which means that frostbite, can be a risk, but this doesn't happen very often.

To conclude, the climatic conditions in for Whistler are excellent for attracting visitors for skiing and snowboarding. The snow conditions and temperature are great motivators.

www.skiing.suite101.com/article.cfm/whistler_blackcomb_weather_december_2008
http://www.whistler.com/stats/
http://www.whistler.world-guides.com/whistle_weather.html

The effects of lack of snow are addressed.

A clear list of sources has been supplied to show websites used in the research.

The task being addressed is clearly identified. For clarity, D2 could have been indicated.

Findings are backed up by facts, and sources have been identified.

Task 3

To: Fran Devlin

From: Jade Falshaw

Report on effect of hurricanes on travel to the Caribbean

Introduction
Tropical storms vary in strength. The strongest ones in the Caribbean are known as hurricanes. All hurricanes are given a name e.g. Gustav, Wilma and Katrina. The hurricane season in the Caribbean lasts from June 1 to November 30. The peak months are August and September. Hurricanes are rated from category 1, which is the mildest with winds of at least 74 mph, to 5 (strongest), with winds over 155mph.

The risk of hurricanes varies in different parts of the Caribbean. Low-risk islands include those in the southern Caribbean e.g. Trinidad and Tobago, Barbados, Grenada, Bonaire and Curacao. According to the Dow Jones Island Index completed in 2006 the islands most at risk of disruption from tropical storms are the Dominican Republic, Cuba, Puerto Rico, Jamaica and St Lucia. Not all Caribbean islands were included in the Dow Jones report, but for the Dominican Republic it stated: 'This island attracts more tourists than most other Caribbean spots; bad risk rating was due to recent flooding and prevalence of hurricanes'.

Hurricanes can affect travel to the Caribbean in different ways, including:
• physical damage and loss of life
• disruption to holidays and travel e.g. airport closures
• stormy weather in the area surrounding the path of the hurricane
• disinclination to book holidays to risk areas during the hurricane season.

This report is going to look at the effect of major hurricanes on the islands of the **Dominican Republic, Cuba** and **Jamaica** as these are popular for holidaymakers from Britain who are attracted by the fantastic beaches and sunshine.

Recent hurricanes
Hurricanes have affected the islands of the Dominican Republic, Cuba and Jamaica every year in recent times. Here are some examples of effects of some of the recent hurricanes:

Ivan 2004
• Tourists airlifted from Jamaica to Dominican Republic.
• British Airways flights cancelled.
• Cuba – flooding.

Wilma 2005
• Flooding in Cuba.
• Evacuation of 625,000 people.
• 13 killed in Jamaica.

Noel 2007
• 160 killed in Dominican Republic.
• Houses completely destroyed, broken bridges and roads.
• No drinking water.

Relevant examples from the last ten years have been identified.

Four key effects have been identified – these are later used to give some structure to the report.

Some analysis is shown.

Gustav 2008
- Called the worst storm since 1956.
- Cuba: heavy flooding and washed out roads, evacuation of over 500,000 people, knocked out electricity and destroyed buildings, tobacco crops ruined.
- Jamaica: airports and transport routes closed by government. Electricity supplies affected. Mass evacuation. Flooding.

Ike 2008
- Damages of $40 million in Cuba (just 10 days after Gustav).
- 1 million evacuated, 7 killed.
- Widespread damage to buildings and roads.
- Crops destroyed.
- Floods in Jamaica.

Dean 2008
- Dominican Republic: 1 died, airports closed, mass evacuations.
- Cuba: tourist programmes suspended, mass evacuations.
- Jamaica: country on full alert, airports closed, 48-hour curfew imposed, evacuations.

There are many more examples of extreme tropical storms hitting these islands (and many other Caribbean destinations e.g. Haiti, Bahamas, Cayman islands), causing similar damage.

Effect of hurricanes on travel to Cuba, Dominican Republic and Jamaica

Physical damage, loss of life
From my research these hurricanes do not seem to have severely affected tourists. There are no reports of loss of life or injury to British tourists to Cuba, Dominican Republic or Jamaica. There are limited reports of physical damage to hotels and tourist resorts. Postings on sites such as TripAdvisor show that in many cases the damage didn't severely affect holiday resorts and there are many reports of good weather at the time of the hurricanes, especially in Jamaica. Some postings do mention physical damage. Here are two separate postings on TripAdvisor on 4 September, four days after Hurricane Gustav hit Cuba in 2008:

'Today we were contacted by our UK tour operator who had been in touch with Cubanacan their agents in Cuba and on Cayo Largo.

We were told that the hotels were opening again this week after a clear up, having suffered little damage, apparently what damage there was caused were to palm trees in hotel grounds.'

'I have been reading a forum (in French) and it appears that the flights to the island resumed on Monday after the hurricane.

One hotel has remained open for business (Club Sol) and the Pelicano will be back in business within one month. As for the Barcelo I am not sure, it suffered the worse damage since the lobby area is all glass'

In most cases if a hotel has suffered physical damage tourists are offered another one so travel plans do not have to be affected. According to Euromonitor, reporting on the Dominican Republic: *'These natural disasters left tourism facilities mostly unaffected, as the major damage was focused in other areas. Reconstruction of the affected areas is in progress and international help has been received'.*

Disruption to holidays and travel
British tour operators, for example Thomas Cook, Virgin Holidays and Cosmos continue to offer holidays to Cuba, Jamaica and the Dominican Republic during the hurricane season. This is what Thomas Cook says in its 2009–2010 brochure, with the main points highlighted:

Different sources of information have been clearly shown in the work.

The brochure extract is relevant and has been clearly referenced.

'**Weather and Natural Disasters**: Destinations featured in this brochure may be affected by weather patterns such as _tropical storms_, monsoons, _hurricanes_, cyclones, typhoons, flooding and also seismic activity causing earthquakes and tidal waves. _An example of which is the 'hurricane season'_, which affects the Atlantic, _Caribbean Sea_ and Gulf of Mexico and is _generally considered to be between June and November_. This is just one example and different weather patterns occur at different times of the year, _their impact on destinations can and does vary_. It's not possible for us to publish detailed information on weather patterns for each destination in our brochure, and _weather advice can frequently change_, we recommend you check the latest FCO Travel Advice for your destination. Visit www.fco.gov.uk/travel for information.

When a _storm or natural disaster occurs, travel and accommodation arrangements may be significantly disrupted_. It is extremely difficult to predict with accuracy the actual path, duration or severe weather patterns and seismic activity may have and the effects of actual or threatened bad weather and natural disasters are beyond our control (please refer to our booking conditions, section "Circumstances Beyond Our Control" for details of our responsibility to you in these circumstances).

If a storm or natural disaster is forecast to affect one of destinations, we work with local and international authorities, our Health and Safety/resort teams and local agents to try to minimise disruption and keep you well informed. It may be that an _evacuation of your resort, or a delay or cancellation of your flight to or from the resort_ may be necessary. In the event of changes to your holiday due to actual or threatened bad weather, we are not able to offer any compensation.'

Source: Thomas Cook Tropical Shores brochure July 2009–October 2010

One of the main things to remember is that it is very easy to track hurricanes. Their movements are tracked by meteorologists so destinations have advance notice when they are in the path of a hurricane. This allows tour operators the chance to postpone flights or offer people alternative holidays. They can also make plans to make sure their guests already in resorts are safe. Disruption to planned travel and holidays is kept to a minimum – changes are only made when absolutely necessary, and usually this is when the Foreign and Commonwealth Office announces that it isn't advisable to travel.

For example, Thomson Holidays airlifted 700 tourists from Jamaica on three emergency flights to the Dominican Republic before Hurricane Ivan struck. Airports can be temporarily closed but are soon brought back into operation when the hurricane has passed, so travel is not greatly affected.

Stormy weather
There are usually reports of heavy wind and rain in areas for miles outside of the path of hurricanes. This will affect excursions, water sports, sun bathing and relaxation, which are the main reasons why people choose to travel to the Caribbean, so although the hurricane doesn't always affect travel it can affect enjoyment and cause complaints.

Disinclination to book holidays to risk areas during the hurricane season
Many British tour operators offer holidays to Cuba, Jamaica and the Dominican Republic during the hurricane season. It does not look as if people are put off travelling to these destinations during the hurricane season because the prices in current holiday brochures are higher in July/ August than in the months outside the hurricane season. This is usual for British tour operators to have higher prices during the school holidays, but if people were not willing to travel to risk areas during the hurricane season prices would be lower to try and encourage them to book. In fact the hotels in the Dominican Republic offer cheaper prices during the hurricane season so it is surprising that British tour operators don't. This shows that there must be a demand for holidays to these destinations even though there might be the risk of hurricanes.

Even though tour operators like Thomas Cook warn about the hurricane season there must be plenty of people willing to book and take a chance that they won't be affected.

Many hotels in the Caribbean now offer a money back guarantee or postpone holidays if a hurricane is due to hit the area. This can help to persuade people to book. Also many of the hotels are all-inclusive and have all entertainment, etc. under one roof, including wet weather activities so holidaymakers don't have to go outside the hotels when the weather is bad.

Further analysis is being shown in different sections.

Sample learner work page 13

The risk of hurricanes doesn't seem to have affected travel to the Dominican Republic and the Caribbean Tourism organisation reported that despite recent hurricanes tourist arrivals in 2007 reached 4.1million people, an increase of 2 per cent over 2006 figures.

Conclusion

According to the National Hurricane Center in Miami (www.nhc.noaa.gov) although a destination might be affected by surrounding winds and storms, there is little risk of a hurricane hitting the same location twice. Tourism is very important to these destinations and as far as possible business continues as normal. Tour operators continue to sell holidays in the hurricane season and people are willing to buy them and take the risk. In the destinations themselves there are incentives to keep travelling to the islands and lots of special offers and deals to try and persuade people to visit the islands during the hurricane season, and particularly during the peak risk months of August and September.

The main effects on travel seem to have been the temporary closure of airports, disruption to electricity and some stormy weather. Maybe British visitors have just been lucky but many seem willing to take the risk as the vast majority of holidays are not affected by hurricanes. Disruption to travel seems to be temporary and localised and it seems that the vast majority of holidays to the Caribbean during the hurricane season suffer little more than a few days of wind and rainy weather, and some don't even have that.

Bibliography:

www.euromonitor.com/Travel_And_Tourism_in_Dominican_Republic
www.forbes.com
www.caribbeannetnews.com
www.guardian.co.uk/
www.travelwithkids.about.com
www.dominicantoday.com
www.online.wsj.com/public/resources/document
www.cubahurricanes.org
www.news.scotsman.com
Thomas Cook Tropical shores brochure

Observation record

The observation report confirms what has been observed and by whom.

Learner name	Jade Falshaw
Qualification	BTEC Level 2 Diploma in Travel and Tourism
Unit number and title	Unit 3: Understanding the Nature and Effects of World Travel

Description of activity undertaken (please be as specific as possible)

Task 1: PowerPoint presentation to colleagues on climatic conditions and their effect on travel to worldwide destinations.

Colleagues present: Fran Devlin (Manager), Josh Long, Chris Lee, Juanita Goncales, Tina Harding, Megan Hinds, Chandra Parikh, Jessica Thorpe

Assessment and grading criteria

P3: describe climatic conditions affecting travel to worldwide destinations, identifying seasonal variations

How the activity meets the requirements of the assessment and grading criteria

Jade made a presentation on four climatic conditions as required: severe tropical storms, snow, sun and monsoons. Comprehensive PowerPoint slides were used to support the presentation.

Jade clarified the difference between hurricanes, typhoons and cyclones and identified where and when they are likely to occur, and in relation to global aspects. Potential effects were described; she summarised how they might affect travel in terms of disruption to travel, damage to buildings etc and gave some hints for potential travellers, such as the best time to travel to avoid hurricanes and getting a cheaper deal if willing to risk travelling in the main hurricane season.

Snow was identified as good for winter sports and this was the main focus when identifying some relevant destinations that rely on snow for the winter sports season in the UK, Europe and worldwide. Typical ski seasons were identified, with the best times to travel, including southern hemisphere. Favourable and less favourable conditions were described, including the effects of too little and too much snow and the actions that have to be taken to counter this. Jade also described what ski resorts might offer the visitor outside the snow season.

Jade's presentation on the sun included also reference to high humidity, excessively high temperatures, southern hemisphere and sun exposure. Distinctions between Mediterranean summer sun and winter sun destinations were made, including examples of worldwide locations. Extreme conditions were included as well as favourable conditions, and possible effects were identified. The presentation concluded with an explanation of the effect of rain and in particular the monsoon rains accompanying the monsoon winds, where and when they occur and the potential effects of these.

Jade had annotated a large world map to support her description. On this she had marked the areas affected by hurricanes, cyclones, typhoons and monsoons, a range of worldwide destinations in both hemispheres that are popular for winter sports, and holiday sunshine spots. She referred to this during her presentation. Jade also used her PowerPoint slides effectively to support her presentation and gave a good insight into four climatic conditions that can affect travel to worldwide destinations. This is a huge subject and her presentation covered the requirements of the P3.

Range addressed within the presentation as a whole:
- four climatic conditions
- potential effect on travel to worldwide destinations
- locations and times of the year to avoid
- locations and times of the year with favourable conditions
- unusual or extreme conditions
- reference to global aspects.

Assessor signature	Fran Devlin	Date	16 December 2010
Assessor name	Fran Devlin		

The report states how the relevant criteria have been addressed.

Assessor's comments

The feedback section provides a useful opportunity for you to reflect on what you enjoyed about an assignment and what you found difficult. Feedback is given for individual criteria and clearly shows which criteria have/ have not been achieved, and why.

The assessor will mark Y (yes) or N (no) to show which criteria have been achieved.

Qualification	BTEC Level 2 Travel and Tourism	Year	2010–2011
Unit number and title	Unit 3: Understanding the Nature and Effects of World Travel	Learner name	Jade Falshaw

Grading criteria	Achieved?
P3 describe climatic conditions affecting travel to worldwide destinations, identifying seasonal variations	Y
M2 explain how seasonal climatic conditions can affect travel to worldwide destinations	N
D2 analyse the effect of extreme or unusual climatic conditions on travel to named worldwide destinations	Y

Learner feedback

I quite liked finding out about the best time to travel to places and when to avoid. It was interesting to research the impact of hurricanes. I enjoyed doing the information sheets but didn't really like having to present in front of the group, but I have got better at this.

Assessor feedback

P3 – see separate observation record for full feedback. A very informative presentation Jade. You gave a very good overview of four climatic conditions and showed how they can affect travel to certain destinations. You have obviously spent a long time on your research and your PowerPoint slides were of an excellent standard. Well done! P3 achieved.

M2 – two destinations with differing climatic conditions have been selected for M2: Dominican Republic and Whistler. You have shown some good independent research here and your sources have been referenced. You have explained how seasonal climatic conditions can affect travel to the Dominican Republic by reducing visitor numbers during the hurricane season. You have shown how the majority of visitors will select the months when better weather is guaranteed, even though hotel rooms and prices are at a premium. You have identified some of the actions taken by hotels, etc to encourage people to travel during the hurricane season. You have met M2 for this part of your explanation.

However you have only explained the winter/spring weather conditions for Whistler. Although it is mainly a winter sports resort and everything you have said about climate is fine, you need to explain what the climate is like at other times of the year; that is, seasonal climatic conditions. This is particularly relevant as you have indicated that over half of the visitors travel to Whistler in the summer. What is it about the climate that attracts people at that time of the year? You need to include seasonal variations in order to fully meet M2. M2 not yet achieved.

D2 – there is evidence of some very good independent research here. You have given an excellent insight into the effects of hurricanes and have used relevant examples from recent years. You have focused on three destinations but have acknowledged that many other Caribbean destinations are also at risk of extreme weather. You have used a variety of sources of information to help you to make some analysis and have shown that, despite the risk, tourism and travel continue to be important to the Caribbean and that for the vast majority of travellers their holiday will not be affected. An exceptionally full report and useful analysis – well done Jade. D2 achieved.

Action plan

You've done really well Jade and you are on target to get an overall distinction grade in this unit, but unless you achieve M2, you will not be able to gain more than a pass grade overall. In order to fully meet M2, please complete the explanation to show how seasonal weather affects travel to Whistler in summer and autumn (it does have a very active tourist industry outside of the winter sports season and climatic conditions at different times of the year must influence this). Additional work to be submitted by 20 January 2011, please. If you need any help with this, please let me know.

Assessor signature	Fran Devlin	Date	6 January 2011
Learner signature	Jade Falshaw	Date	7 January 2011

The action plan is important as it will confirm areas for improvement for criteria not yet achieved or for working towards higher grades.

Coping with problems

TOP TIPS

If you have a serious complaint or concern, talk to your chosen tutor first – for example, if you believe an assignment grade is unfair. All centres have official procedures to cover important issues such as appeals about assignments and formal complaints, but it's usually sensible to try to resolve a problem informally first.

Most learners sail through their BTEC First with no major problems. Unfortunately, not everyone is so lucky. Some may have personal difficulties or other issues that disrupt their work so they are late handing in their assignments. If this happens to you, it's vital to know what to do. This checklist should help.

Checklist for coping with problems

- ✔ Check that you know who to talk to.

- ✔ Don't sit on a problem and worry about it. Talk to someone promptly, in confidence. It's always easier to cope if you've shared it with someone.

- ✔ Most centres have professional counsellors you can talk to if you prefer. They won't repeat anything you say to them without your permission.

- ✔ If you've done something wrong or silly, people will respect you more if you are honest, admit where you went wrong and apologise promptly.

Case study: Talking about problems

Harvey made a great start to his BTEC First in Travel and Tourism and was on target to gain at least a merit overall, maybe even a distinction. However at the start of the third term of his course things started to go wrong.

'My dad lost his job and things became very difficult at home. Mum and dad wouldn't talk about it with me, but said money was going to be tight now so I extended my hours at work.

'I got very tired working extra shifts and my college work began to suffer. Sometimes I missed sessions at college. My friends moaned that I wasn't pulling my weight in the group assessment we were working on. I didn't want to tell them what was going on at home and they were annoyed when our group was referred on a presentation because I hadn't done my part of the research properly.

'I felt really fed up. Eventually I had a big row with another member of the group and I thought I would be disciplined by my tutor. I ended up telling my tutor everything and I just wish I had told her earlier because it took a great weight off my shoulders. She helped me to put together an action plan to catch up on late work and encouraged me to talk to my parents.

'Eventually I told mum and dad that I was having problems at college. Together we worked out that I could cut down on the shifts I was doing at work and I started to get back on track to successfully complete my course.'

Do you think Harvey would have completed his course if things had not come to a head and he decided to talk to his tutor?

Skills building

To do your best in your assignments you need a number of skills, including:

- your **personal, learning and thinking skills**
- your **functional skills** of ICT, mathematics and English
- your proofreading and document-production skills.

Personal, learning and thinking skills (PLTS)

These are the skills, personal qualities and behaviour that you find in people who are effective and confident at work. These people enjoy carrying out a wide range of tasks, always try to do their best, and work well alone or with others. They enjoy a challenge and use new experiences to learn and develop.

Activity: How good are your PLTS?

1 Do this quiz to help you identify areas for improvement.

a) I get on well with other people.

Always   Usually   Seldom   Never

b) I try to find out other people's suggestions for solving problems that puzzle me.

Always   Usually   Seldom   Never

c) I plan carefully to make sure I meet my deadlines.

Always   Usually   Seldom   Never

d) If someone is being difficult, I think carefully before making a response.

Always   Usually   Seldom   Never

e) I don't mind sharing my possessions or my time.

Always   Usually   Seldom   Never

f) I take account of other people's views and opinions.

Always   Usually   Seldom   Never

g) I enjoy thinking of new ways of doing things.

Always   Usually   Seldom   Never

h) I like creating new and different things.

Always   Usually   Seldom   Never

i) I enjoy planning and finding ways of solving problems.

Always   Usually   Seldom   Never

j) I enjoy getting feedback about my performance.

Always   Usually   Seldom   Never

k) I try to learn from constructive criticism so that I know what to improve.

Always   Usually   Seldom   Never

l) I enjoy new challenges.

Always   Usually   Seldom   Never

m) I am even-tempered.

Always   Usually   Seldom   Never

n) I am happy to make changes when necessary.

Always   Usually   Seldom   Never

o) I like helping other people.

Always   Usually   Seldom   Never

Score 3 points for each time you answered 'Always', 2 points for 'Usually', 1 point for 'Seldom' and 0 points for 'Never'. The higher your score, the higher your personal, learning and thinking skills.

2 How creative are you? Test yourself with this activity. Identify 50 different objects you could fit into a matchbox at the same time! As a start, three suitable items are a postage stamp, a grain of rice, a staple. Can you find 47 more?

BTEC FACTS

Your BTEC First qualification is at Level 2. Qualifications in functional skills start at Entry level and continue to Level 2. (You don't need to achieve functional skills to gain any BTEC qualification, and the evidence from a BTEC assignment can't be used towards the assessment of functional skills.)

Functional skills

Functional skills are the practical skills you need to function confidently, effectively and independently at work, when studying and in everyday life. They focus on the following areas:

- Information and Communications Technology (ICT)
- Maths
- English.

You may already be familiar with functional skills. Your BTEC First tutors will give you more information about how you will continue to develop these skills on your new course.

ICT skills

These will relate directly to how much 'hands-on' practice you have had on IT equipment. You may be an experienced IT user, and using word-processing, spreadsheet and presentation software may be second nature. Searching for information online may be something you do every day – in between downloading music, buying or selling on eBay and updating your Facebook profile!

Or you may prefer to avoid computer contact as much as possible. If so, there are two things you need to do.

1   Use every opportunity to improve your ICT skills so that you can start to live in the 21st century!

2   Make life easier by improving your basic proofreading and document preparation skills.

Proofreading and document preparation skills

Being able to produce well-displayed work quickly will make your life a lot easier. On any course there will be at least one unit that requires you to use good document preparation skills.

Tips to improve your document production skills

✔   If your keyboarding skills are poor, ask if there is a workshop you can join. Or your library or resource centre may have software you can use.

✔   Check that you know the format of documents you have to produce for assignments. It can help to have a 'model' version of each type in your folder for quick reference.

✔   Practise checking your work by reading word by word – and remember not to rely on spellcheckers (see page 62).

Activity: How good are your ICT skills?

1a)   Test your current ICT abilities by responding *honestly* to each of the following statements.

i)   I can create a copy of my timetable using a word-processing or spreadsheet package.
True   False

ii)   I can devise and design a budget for myself for the next three months using a spreadsheet package.
True   False

iii)   I can email a friend who has just got broadband to say how to minimise the danger of computer viruses, what a podcast is and also explain the restrictions on music downloads.
True   False

iv)   I can use presentation software to prepare a presentation containing four or five slides on a topic of my choice.
True   False

v)   I can research online to compare the performance and prices of laptop computers, and prepare an information sheet using word-processing software.
True   False

vi)   I can prepare a poster, with graphics, for my mother's friend, who is starting her own business preparing children's party food, and attach it to an email to her for approval.
True   False

TRY THIS

Learning to touch type can save you hours of time. Go to page 106 to find out how to access a website where you can check your keyboarding skills.

TOP TIPS

Print your work on good paper and keep it flat so that it looks good when you hand it in.

1b) Select any one of the above to which you answered false and learn how to do it.

2 Compare the two tables below. The first is an original document; the second is a typed copy. Are they identical? Highlight any differences you find and check them with the key on page 105.

Name	Date	Time	Room
Abbott	16 July	9.30 am	214
Grey	10 August	10.15 am	160
Johnston	12 August	2.20 pm	208
Waverley	18 July	3.15 pm	180
Jackson	30 September	11.15 am	209
Gregory	31 August	4.20 pm	320
Marshall	10 September	9.30 am	170
Bradley	16 September	2.20 pm	210

Name	Date	Time	Room
Abbott	26 July	9.30 am	214
Gray	10 August	10.15 am	160
Johnson	12 August	2.20 pm	208
Waverley	18 July	3.15 am	180
Jackson	31 September	11.15 am	209
Gregory	31 August	4.20 pm	320
Marshall	10 September	9.30 pm	170
Bradley	16 August	2.20 pm	201

Maths or numeracy skills

Four easy ways to improve your numeracy skills

1 Work out simple calculations in your head, like adding up the prices of items you are buying. Then check if you are correct when you pay for them.

2 Set yourself numeracy problems based on your everyday life. For example, if you are on a journey that takes 35 minutes and you leave home at 11.10 am, what time will you arrive? If you are travelling at 40 miles an hour, how long will it take you to go 10 miles?

3 Treat yourself to a Maths Training program.

4 Check out online sites to improve your skills. Go to page 106 to find out how to access a useful BBC website.

TOP TIPS

Quickly test answers. For example, if fuel costs 85p a litre and someone is buying 15 litres, estimate this at £1 x 15 (£15) and the answer should be just below this. So if your answer came out at £140, you'd immediately know you'd done something wrong!

Activity: How good are your maths skills?

Answer as many of the following questions as you can in 15 minutes. Check your answers with the key on page 105.

1 **a)** 12 + 28 = ?

   i) 30   ii) 34   iii) 38   iv) 40   v) 48

b) 49 ÷ 7 = ?

   i) 6   ii) 7   iii) 8   iv) 9   v) 10

c) ½ + 1¼ = ?

   i) ¾   ii) 1½   iii) 1¾   iv) 2¼   v) 3

d) 4 × 12 = 8 × ?

   i) 5   ii) 6   iii) 7   iv) 8   v) 9

e) 16.5 + 25.25 − ? = 13.25

   i) 28.5   ii) 31.25 iii) 34.5 iv) 41.65 v) 44

2 **a)** You buy four items at £1.99, two at 98p and three at £1.75. You hand over a £20 note. How much change will you get? _____

b) What fraction of one litre is 250 ml? _____

c) What percentage of £50 is £2.50? _____

d) A designer travelling on business can claim 38.2p a mile in expenses. How much is she owed if she travels 625 miles? _____

e) You are flying to New York in December. New York is five hours behind British time and the flight lasts eight hours. If you leave at 11.15 am, what time will you arrive? _____

f) For your trip to the United States you need American dollars. You find that the exchange rate is $1.5 dollars.

   i)   How many dollars will you receive if you exchange £500? _____

   ii) Last year your friend visited New York when the exchange rate was $1.8. She also exchanged £500. Did she receive more dollars than you or fewer – and by how much? _____

g) A security guard and his dog patrol the perimeter fence of a warehouse each evening. The building is 480 metres long and 300 metres wide and the fence is 80 metres out from the building on all sides. If the guard and his dog patrol the fence three times a night, how far will they walk? _____

English skills

Your English skills affect your ability to understand what you read, prepare a written document, say what you mean and understand other people. Even if you're doing a practical subject, there will always be times when you need to leave someone a note, tell them about a phone call, read or listen to instructions – or write a letter for a job application!

Six easy ways to improve your English skills

1   Read more. It increases the number of words you know and helps to make you familiar with correct spellings.

2   Look up words you don't understand in a dictionary and check their meaning. Then try to use them yourself to increase your vocabulary.

3   Do crosswords. These help increase your vocabulary and practise your spelling at the same time.

4   You can use websites to help you get to grips with English vocabulary, grammar and punctuation. Go to page 106 to find out how to access a useful BBC website.

5   Welcome opportunities to practise speaking in class, in discussion groups and during presentations – rather than avoiding them!

6   Test your ability to listen to someone else by seeing how much you can remember when they've finished speaking.

Activity: How good are your English skills?

1   In the table below are 'wrong' versions of words often spelled incorrectly. Write the correct spellings on the right. Check your list against the answers on page 105.

Incorrect spelling	Correct spelling
accomodation	
seperate	
definate	
payed	
desparate	
acceptible	
competant	
succesful	

2 Correct the error(s) in these sentences.

   a) The plug on the computer is lose.

   b) The car was stationery outside the house.

   c) Their going on they're holidays tomorrow.

   d) The principle of the college is John Smith.

   e) We are all going accept Tom.

3 Punctuate these sentences correctly.

   a) Toms train was late on Monday and Tuesday.

   b) She is going to France Belgium Spain and Italy in the summer.

   c) He comes from Leeds and says its great there.

4 Read the article on copyright.

Copyright

Anyone who uses a photocopier can break copyright law if they carry out unrestricted photocopying of certain documents. This is because The Copyright, Designs and Patents Act 1988 protects the creator of an original work against having it copied without permission.

Legally, every time anyone writes a book, composes a song, makes a film or creates any other type of artistic work, this work is treated as their property (or copyright). If anyone else wishes to make use of it, they must get permission to do so and, on occasions, pay a fee.

Licences can be obtained to allow educational establishments to photocopy limited numbers of some publications. In addition, copies of an original document can be made for certain specific purposes. These include research and private study. Under the Act, too, if an article is summarised and quoted by anyone, then the author and title of the original work must be acknowledged.

a) Test your ability to understand unfamiliar information by responding to the following statements with 'True' or 'False'.

i) Students and tutors in schools and colleges can copy anything they want.
True   False

ii) The law which covers copyright is The Copyright, Designs and Patents Act 1988.
True   False

iii) A student photocopying a document in the library must have a licence.
True   False

iv) Copyright only relates to books in the library.
True   False

v) If you quote a newspaper report in an assignment, you don't need to state the source.
True   False

vii) Anyone is allowed to photocopy a page of a book for research purposes.
True   False

b) Make a list of key points in the article, then write a brief summary in your own words.

5 Nikki has read a newspaper report that a horse racing in the Kentucky Derby had to be put down. The filly collapsed and the vet couldn't save her. Nikki says it's the third time in two years a racehorse has had to be put down in the US. As a horse lover she is convinced racing should be banned in Britain and the US. She argues that fox hunting was banned to protect foxes, and that racehorses are more important and more expensive than foxes. Darren disagrees. He says the law is not working, hardly anyone has been prosecuted and fox hunting is going on just like before. Debbie says that animals aren't important whilst there is famine in the world.

a) Do you think the three arguments are logical? See if you can spot the flaws and check your ideas with the suggestions on page 105.

b) Sporting activities and support for sporting teams often provoke strong opinions. For a sport or team of your choice, identify two opposing views that might be held. Then decide how you would give a balanced view. Test your ideas with a friend or family member.

Answers

Skills building answers

ICT activities

2 Differences between the two tables are highlighted in bold.

Name	Date	Time	Room
Abbott	**16** July	9.30 am	214
Grey	10 August	10.15 am	160
Johnston	12 August	2.20 pm	208
Waverley	18 July	3.15 **pm**	180
Jackson	**30** September	11.15 am	209
Gregory	31 August	4.20 pm	320
Marshall	10 September	9.30 **am**	170
Bradley	16 **September**	2.20 pm	**210**

Maths/numeracy activities

1 **a)** iv, **b)** ii, **c)** iii, **d)** ii, **e)** i

2 **a)** £4.83, **b)** ¼, **c)** 5%, **d)** £238.75, **e)** 2.15 pm, **f)** **i)** $750 **ii)** $150 dollars more, **g)** 6.6 km.

English activities

1 Spellings: accommodation, separate, definite, paid, desperate, acceptable, competent, successful

2 Errors:
a) The plug on the computer is <u>loose</u>.
b) The car was <u>stationary</u> outside the house.
c) <u>They're</u> going on <u>their</u> holidays tomorrow.
d) The <u>principal</u> of the college is John Smith.
e) We are all going <u>except</u> Tom.

3 Punctuation:
a) Tom's train was late on Monday and Tuesday.
b) She is going to France, Belgium, Spain and Italy in the summer.
c) He comes from Leeds and says it's great there.

4 **a) i)** False, **ii)** True, **iii)** False, **iv)** False, **v)** False, **vi)** False, **vii)** True

5 A logical argument would be that if racehorses are frequently injured in a particular race, eg one with difficult jumps, then it should not be held. It is not logical to compare racehorses with foxes. The value of the animal is irrelevant if you are assessing cruelty. Darren's argument is entirely different and unrelated to Nikki's. Whether or not fox hunting legislation is effective or not has no bearing on the danger (or otherwise) to racehorses. Finally, famine is a separate issue altogether. You cannot logically 'rank' problems in the world to find a top one and ignore the others until this is solved!

Accessing website links

Links to various websites are referred to throughout this BTEC Level 2 First Study Skills Guide. In order to ensure that these links are up to date, that they work and that the sites aren't inadvertently linked to any material that could be considered offensive, we have made the links available on our website: www.pearsonhotlinks.co.uk. When you visit the site, search for either the title BTEC Level 2 First Study Skills Guide in Travel and Tourism or the ISBN 9781846905674 to gain access to the website links and information on how they can be used to help you with your studies.

Useful terms

Apprenticeships
Schemes that enable you to work and earn money at the same time as you gain further qualifications (an NVQ award and a technical certificate) and improve your functional skills. Apprentices learn work-based skills relevant to their job role and their chosen industry. See page 106 for information on how to access a link where you can find out more.

Assessment methods
Methods, such as practical tasks and assignments, which are used to check that your work demonstrates the learning and understanding you need to obtain the qualification.

Assessor
The tutor who marks or assesses your work.

Assignment
A complete task or mini-**project** set to meet specific grading criteria.

Assignment brief
The information and instructions related to a particular assignment.

BTEC Level 3 Nationals
Qualifications you can take when you have successfully achieved a Level 2 qualification, such as BTEC First. They are offered in a variety of subjects.

Credit value
The number of credits attached to your BTEC course. The credit value increases relative to the length of time you need to complete the course, from 15 credits for a BTEC Certificate, to 30 credits for a BTEC Extended Certificate and 60 credits for a BTEC Diploma.

Command word
The word in an assignment that tells you what you have to do to produce the type of answer that is required, eg 'list', 'describe', 'analyse'.

Educational Maintenance Award (EMA)
This is a means-tested award which provides eligible learners under 19 who are studying a full-time course at a centre with a cash sum of money every week. See page 106 for information on how to access a link where you can find out more.

Functional skills
The practical skills that enable all learners to use and apply English, Maths and ICT both at work and in their everyday lives. They aren't compulsory to achieve on the course, but are of great use to you.

Grade
The rating of pass, merit or distinction that is given to an assignment you have completed, which identifies the standard you have achieved.

Grading criteria
The standard you have to demonstrate to obtain a particular grade in the unit. In other words, what you have to prove you can do.

Grading grid
The table in each unit of your BTEC qualification specification that sets out the grading criteria.

Indicative reading
Recommended books, magazines, journals and websites whose content is both suitable and relevant to the unit.

Induction
A short programme of events at the start of a course or work placement designed to give you essential information and introduce you to other people so that you can settle in easily.

Internal verification
The quality checks carried out by nominated tutors at all centres to ensure that all assignments are at the right level and cover appropriate learning outcomes. The checks also ensure that all **assessors** are marking work consistently and to the same standards.

Learning outcomes

The learning and skills you must demonstrate to show that you have learned a unit effectively.

Levels of study

The depth, breadth and complexity of knowledge, understanding and skills required to achieve a qualification determines its level. Level 2 is equivalent to GCSE level (grades A* to C). Level 3 equates to GCE A-level. As you successfully achieve one level, you can progress on to the next. BTEC qualifications are offered at Entry Level, then Levels 1, 2, 3, 4, 5, 6 and 7.

Mandatory units

On a BTEC Level 2 First course, these are the compulsory units that all learners must complete to gain the qualification.

Optional units

Units on your course from which you may be able to make a choice. They help you specialise your skills, knowledge and understanding, and may help progression into work or further education.

Personal, learning and thinking skills (PLTS)

The skills and qualities that improve your ability to work independently and be more effective and confident at work. Opportunities for developing these are a feature of all BTEC First courses. They aren't compulsory to achieve on the course, but are of great use to you.

Plagiarism

Copying someone else's work or work from any other sources (eg the internet) and passing it off as your own. It is strictly forbidden on all courses.

Portfolio

A collection of work compiled by a learner – for an **assessor** – usually as evidence of learning.

Project

A comprehensive piece of work which normally involves original research and planning and investigation either by an individual or a team. The outcome will vary depending upon the type of project undertaken. For example, it may result in the organisation of a specific event, a demonstration of a skill, a presentation, or a piece of writing.

Tutorial

An individual or small group meeting with your tutor at which you discuss the work you are currently doing and other more general course issues.

Unit content

Details about the topics covered by the unit and the knowledge and skills you need to complete it.

Work placement

Time spent on an employer's premises when you carry out work-based tasks as an employee and also learn about the enterprise to develop your skills and knowledge.

Work-related qualification

A qualification designed to help you to develop the knowledge and understanding you need for a particular area of work.